ATHENS

KATERINA SERVI
Archaeologist

EKDOTIKE ATHENON S.A.
Athens 2009

Publisher: Ghristiana G. Christopoulou
Editor of texts and ilustrations: Katerina Servi
Layout: Irini Kaloyera
Cover design: Angela Simou
Colour reproduction, printing and binding:
METRON S.A.-Ekdotike Hellados
Translation and proofreading:
Alexandra Doumas

ISBN 978-960-213-389-7
Copyright © 2000 Ekdotike Athenon S.A.
13, Ippokratous St., Athens 106 72

CONTENTS

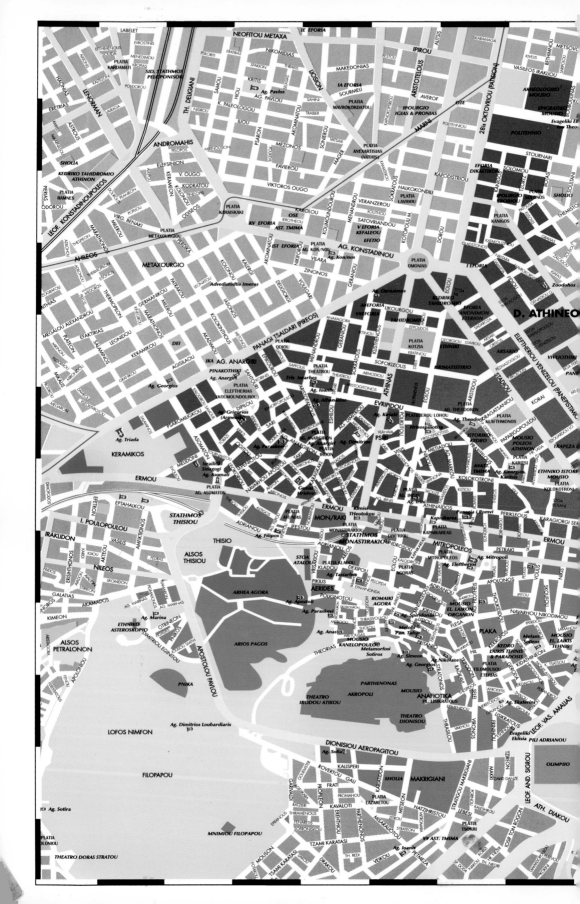

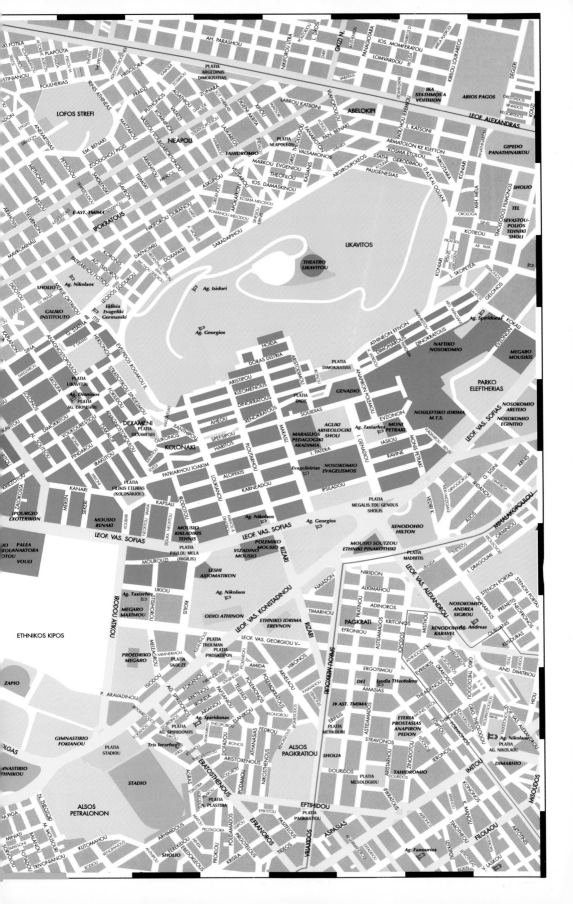

THE HISTORY OF ATHENS

Mycenaean warriors whose feats passed into the sphere of myth. Orators and philosophers whose words were more powerful than the armies of Persia. Sculptors and architects who made stone come to life. Byzantine painters who imprinted their faith in churches and monasteries. Men and women who revolted against their oppressors and won their freedom, in order to found a modern democratic state. People who lived and created in different phases of history. People who for thousands of years have shared the same land, the same language, the same incomparable Attic sky.

The goddess Athena, patron deity of Athens, was frequently given the epithet Promachos because she helped men in battle and in difficult moments generally. Bronze votive statuette of Athena Promachos, from the Acropolis, c. 480-470 BC. Athens, National Archaeological Museum.

PREHISTORIC - GEOMETRIC TIMES

The history of Athens is the history of a city whose birth is lost in the mists of time. The earliest traces of habitation date back to the Neolithic Age. Later, in the 2nd millennium BC, Ionians from northwest Thessaly migrated southwards and some of them settled in Attica. There they mixed and married with the local inhabitants, traditionally referred to as Pelasgians. During the Mycenaean period (1600-1100 BC) the city was the seat of a king. His palace and the residences of his nobles were built on the Acropolis, which was fortified with enormous walls, called Cyclopean, after the mid-13th century BC. In the latter years of the same century Mycenaean monarchs from all over Greece joined forces in a campaign against Troy.

According to mythology, the cause of the Trojan War was the abduction of Helen, wife of Menelaos King of Sparta, by Paris, son of the King of Troy. Here Paris leads Helen to his ship. Aphrodite, behind Helen, covers her with the bridal veil, while Eros, in front of Helen, arranges her diadem. Red-figure skyphos, c. 480 BC. Boston, Museum of Fine Arts.

The Athenians also took part in the protracted hostilities of the Trojan War. Homer mentions that 50 Athenian ships led by King Menestheus sped to reinforce the fleet of Agamemnon, king of 'gold-rich' Mycenae.
After the descent of the Dorians in the late 12th century BC and the break up of the Mycenaean world, the small communities existing in Attica united into a single city with a common bouleuterion and prytaneion. The Athenians of the Classical period believed that this synoecism was achieved on the initiative of the mythical king Theseus. In order to symbolize the new political unity Theseus is said to have renamed the Athenaia, the great festival in honour of the goddess Athena, the Panathenaia. From that period already Athens was divided into two parts: the Acropolis, in which the city's main sanctuaries were concentrated, and the *asty*, where the houses and the Agora were located.

During the Geometric period – which is so named because of the use of geometric motifs in vase decoration – Athens emerged as an important centre of trade and art.

ARCHAIC TIMES

In the ensuing centuries the foundations were laid for the city's great political and cultural floruit. By the end of the 7th century BC the institution of kingship was defunct and the Athenian body politic had developed into an Aristocracy. This regime was partially changed by Drakon, who granted political rights to a broader spectrum of Athenians. He also codified the laws, making provision for severe punishments for those who broke them – traditionally known as 'Draconian'. A period of social instability followed, on account of the debts encumbering the farmers. In the early 6th century BC Solon appeared on the political stage. His extremely significant governmental and legislative reforms restored normality and formed the bases of perhaps the greatest creation of the Greek spirit; the Athenian Democracy. Concurrently the city expanded and was surrounded by walls, the Acropolis was dedicated exclusively to cult, while economic

▶

Part of an Attic Geometric krater which had been set up as a marker on the tomb of an Athenian nobleman. 745-740 BC. Athens, National Archaeological Museum.

development led to a burgeoning of the Arts and Letters.

From around the mid-6th century to 527 BC the history of Athens is linked with Peisistratos. Although he usurped power as a tyrant, he ruled with moderation and contributed to the city's economic and intellectual progress. The end of this century was marked by the radical reforms of yet another distinguished legislator, Kleisthenes.

The 5th century BC dawned with the wars between the Greeks and the Persians. The first round of bloody clashes ended with the Athenians' victory at Marathon in 490/89 BC, thanks to the ingenuity of the general Miltiades. After Miltiades' death new political figures dominated the life of Athens. among them Aristeides 'the Just', renowned for his faith in justice and kindly character, and the far-sighted Themistokles. The latter played a decisive role in. the course of the Persians' new campaign against Greece in 480-479 BC. After the battle at the defile of Thermopylae, in which the few hundred Spartan defenders were slain to a man, the Persian army marched through Boeotia into Attica.

In the face of this danger Themistokles managed to persuade the Athenians to abandon their homes. When the enemy invaded Athens they found a deserted city, which they pillaged and burnt down its sanctuaries. In the end the Greek victory in the naval battle of Salamis, where Themistokles distinguished himself as a general, and in the battle of Plataeae, forced the defeated Persians to beat a hasty retreat. In subsequent years Athens spread beyond its old boundaries and was fortified with a new wall, the so-called Themistokleian Wall. For defensive reasons it was also connected with the Piraeus, with the building of the Long Walls.

CLASSICAL TIMES

The end of the Persian Wars marked the beginning of one of the most remarkable periods in the history of mankind. The so-called 'Golden Age' of Athens. The democratic system of government was completed with the reforms of Ephialtes and the most towering of all the Athenian leaders, Pericles. Concurrently, because of the wonderful stability Democracy achieved, philosophers, writers and artists gravitated to the city from all parts of the Hellenic world. Fifth-century BC Athens, the cultural metropolis of the age, opened up radical new highways in every sector of art and thought. In architecture and sculpture with the creators of the Parthenon, in rhetoric with Lysias, in painting and vase-painting, in historiography with Thucydides who recorded every facet of the Peloponnesian War, and above all in theatre, with the dramatic poets

Aeschylus, Sophocles, Euripides and Aristophanes, and philosophy, which received the catalytic influence of the Sophists and of Socrates. This same period saw the birth of the Athenian League, in which a host of cities, from the Aegean islands to the Asia Minor littoral and the Propontis, participated. Slowly but surely however, the League, whose original aim was defensive or offensive war against the Persians, was transformed into a hegemony of Athens. This fact brought the city into conflict with the other great power of the age, Sparta. It was not long before the fiercest of all the civil wars broke out, the Peloponnesian War. Hostilities lasted for 27 years, from 431 until 404 BC, and ended with the 'pyrrhic' victory of Sparta, since both sides had essentially been destroyed.

In the 4th century BC another power, the kingdom of Macedon, took over the helm in Greece. The defeat of the Athenians by Philip II (father of Alexander the Great) at Chaironeia in 338 BC, signalled their city's political decline. Nevertheless cultural activity continued unabated, and in this century personalities of international repute lived, worked and taught in Athens, among them the orators Isokrates, Demosthenes and Lykourgos, the sculptor Praxiteles, the historian Xenophon, the philosophers Plato, pupil of Socrates and founder of his own philosophical school, the Academy

(388 BC), and Aristotle, pupil of Plato and founder of the other renowned school, the Lyceum (335 BC).

In 336 BC one of Aristotle's pupils, the King of Macedon Alexander the Great, set out on his victorious military expeditions. Within a few years he reached the depths of Asia and created a vast empire in which the Greek language and Greek culture were the predominant elements.

HELLENISTIC AND ROMAN TIMES

When Alexander the Great died in 323 BC Athens became an arena of rivalries between his successors. Even so, throughout the Hellenistic period there was considerable building activity, due the benefactions of the kings-heirs to Alexander. Antiochos Epiphanes, Attalos II, Eumenes II filled the city with stoas and gymnasia, and the Acropolis with *ex-votos*.

The heyday of the Hellenistic kingdoms was followed by their gradual conquest by Rome, which was completed in 30 BC

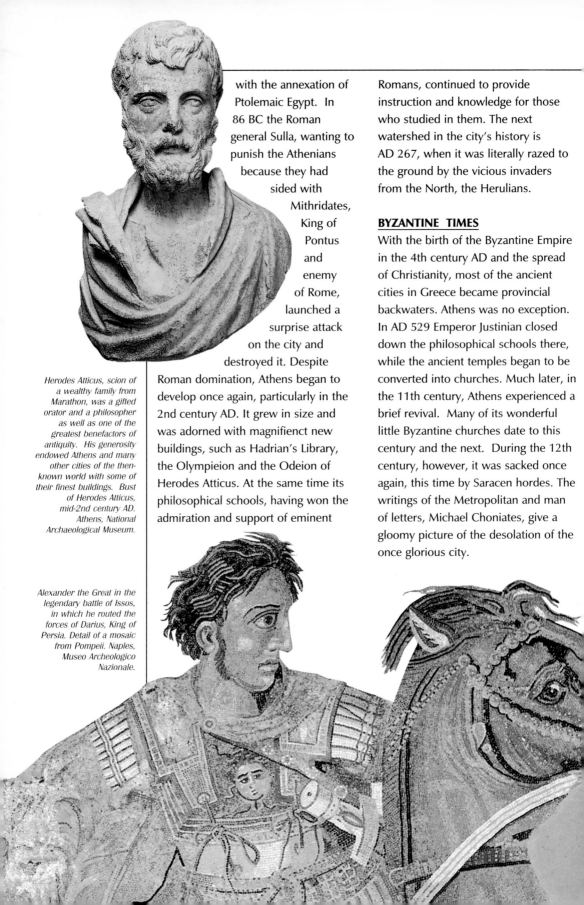

with the annexation of Ptolemaic Egypt. In 86 BC the Roman general Sulla, wanting to punish the Athenians because they had sided with Mithridates, King of Pontus and enemy of Rome, launched a surprise attack on the city and destroyed it. Despite Roman domination, Athens began to develop once again, particularly in the 2nd century AD. It grew in size and was adorned with magnifienct new buildings, such as Hadrian's Library, the Olympieion and the Odeion of Herodes Atticus. At the same time its philosophical schools, having won the admiration and support of eminent Romans, continued to provide instruction and knowledge for those who studied in them. The next watershed in the city's history is AD 267, when it was literally razed to the ground by the vicious invaders from the North, the Herulians.

BYZANTINE TIMES

With the birth of the Byzantine Empire in the 4th century AD and the spread of Christianity, most of the ancient cities in Greece became provincial backwaters. Athens was no exception. In AD 529 Emperor Justinian closed down the philosophical schools there, while the ancient temples began to be converted into churches. Much later, in the 11th century, Athens experienced a brief revival. Many of its wonderful little Byzantine churches date to this century and the next. During the 12th century, however, it was sacked once again, this time by Saracen hordes. The writings of the Metropolitan and man of letters, Michael Choniates, give a gloomy picture of the desolation of the once glorious city.

Herodes Atticus, scion of a wealthy family from Marathon, was a gifted orator and a philosopher as well as one of the greatest benefactors of antiquity. His generosity endowed Athens and many other cities of the then-known world with some of their finest buildings. Bust of Herodes Atticus, mid-2nd century AD. Athens, National Archaeological Museum.

Alexander the Great in the legendary battle of Issos, in which he routed the forces of Darius, King of Persia. Detail of a mosaic from Pompeii. Naples, Museo Archeologico Nazionale.

On 12 April 1204 Constantinople, capital of Byzantium, was captured by the armies of the Fourth Crusade. When the Crusaders divided the Byzantine territories between them, Athens was ceded to Otto della Roche, son of a Burgundian nobleman. It passed successively to other conquerors, such as the Catalans, the Florentine Acciajuoli family and the Venetians. During these years the Acropolis became a mighty fortress once again, the Propylaia was converted into a palace of the foreign governors, the Erechtheion into a residence and the Parthenon into a church, first Greek Orthodox and then Roman Catholic.

In 1261 the Byzantines won back Constantinople, but Athens failed to rid herself of the Latin dynasts.

OTTOMAN RULE - THE GREEK WAR OF INDEPENDENCE

The thousand- year history of the Byzantine Empire finally ended in May 1453, when Constantinople fell to the Ottoman Turks. Three years later, in 1456, the Ottomans entered Athens, where they were to remain for almost four centuries. The city's aspect changed yet again. The Acropolis filled with houses, the Parthenon was converted into a mosque, while below, in the area of the Roman Agora and Hadrian's Library, the administrative centre and the bazaar were created. Mosques, tekes (Dervish monasteries) and bath-houses were built here too. Although so many centuries had passed, the Parthenon was preserved intact, at least externally. And so it was until the Venetian-Turkish wars broke out in the 17th century.

In 1687 the Venetians, led by Morosini, besieged the Acropolis. During the siege a Venetian shell fell on the temple, which the Turks were using as a gunpowder store, and a large part of it was blown up.

The most important event in the history of later Hellenism, the Greek War of Independence, was

Ioannis Capodistrias, first president of Greece, placed his political and diplomatic skills in the service of the country's interests. He was assassinated, however, in September 1831, leaving behind an unfillable void. Painting by D.Tsokos. Athens, National Historical Museum.

The arrival of Otto in Athens, on 1 December 1834, was accompanied by a thanksgiving service celebrated in the church of St George, the ancient temple of Hephaistos. Oil-painting by Peter von Hess, 1835. Munich, Neue Pinakothek.

declared in March 1821. Virtually from the outset, Athens and mainly the Acropolis became a battleground between Greeks and Turks. On 10 June 1822, after an obdurate siege, the Greeks captured the sacred rock and liberated the city.

However, a few years later the situation was reversed. In the summer of 1826 the Turkish army under Kiutahi besieged the Acropolis again. Its Greek defenders were forced to surrender in May 1827.

RECENT TIMES

Despite these setbacks, the Greeks were victorious in their Struggle for Freedom. In February 1830 an independent Greek state was founded. Its first king was Otto, son of Ludwig of Bavaria, who arrived in Greece in 1833. On his decision Athens was nominated capital of the fledgeling Greek state, towards the end of

1834. This set a building boom in motion. The first town plan of Athens was prepared by the Greek architect St. Kleanthis in collaboration with his German colleague E. Schaubert. This was subsequently revised by Leo von Klenze. During the reigns of Otto and George I (1862- 1913) Greek and foreign architects filled the city with public and private buildings. Their works, inspired by the two major

One of the most tragic events in the 1821 War of Independence was the destruction of Chios. Thousands of the island's inhabitants were slain or taken captive, a terrible blow to revolutionary Greece which fired the philhellenic movement throughout Europe. 'The Massacre of Chios', by the French painter E. Delacroix. Paris, Musée du Louvre.

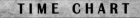

LATE NEOLITHIC PERIOD (4000-2800/2700 BC)
First signs of habitation.

BRONZE AGE (2800/2700-1100 BC)
Descent of the Ionians. Athens part of the Mycenaean world.
Descent of the Dorians.

PROTOGEOMETRIC/GEOMETRIC PERIOD (10th-8th century BC)
A heyday for art and trade.

ARCHAIC PERIOD (7th-6th century BC)
Reforms of Drakon - Solon - Kleisthenes.
Development of Arts and Letters.
Persian Wars.

CLASSICAL PERIOD (479-323 BC)
'Golden Age' of Athens.
Major projects on the Acropolis under Pericles.
The Peloponnesian War marks the beginning of decline.

HELLENISTIC PERIOD (323-30 BC)
Athens' political power weakens.
Intellectual and artistic
creativity continues.

ROMAN AGE (30 BC-AD 330)
Athens still an illustrious cultural centre.
Adorned with magnificent new buildings.

BYZANTINE AGE (330-1453)
Athens a backwater, plagued by incursions
and ruled by the Latins.

OTTOMAN RULE (1453-1821)
Athens a part of the Ottoman Empire.
Great destruction of the Parthenon.

RECENT TIMES
Liberation of Greece from the Turks.
Athens declared capital of the newly-founded Greek state.

The old Military Hospital in Makryyanni street, one of the first public buildings in the capital, was erected in the period 1834-1836 by the German engineer W. von Weiler. It now houses the Acropolis Study Centre. Athens, National Historical Museum.

▶
On 28 October 1940 the Italian ambassador handed the Greek Prime Minister Ioannis Metaxas an ultimatum, demanding the surrender of Greek strategic positions to Italian troops. The historic 'No' (Ochi) of Metaxas's refusal was enthusiastically received by all Greeks. Photograph of a demonstration by the people of Athens on the morning of 28 October. Athens, War Museum.

movements in 19th-century European architecture, Neoclassicism and Romanticism, are the most admirable monuments of later Athens.

After the end of World War I the Greeks tried to conquer part of Asia Minor. The campaign ended catastrophically in 1922, with the destruction of Smyrna by the Turks and the violent expulsion of the Greeks from Asia Minor. There was an enormous influx of refugees to Athens, creating a serious housing crisis, and the city began to spread. After World War II and the Civil War, a new city began to emerge from the ruins. At the same time large-scale population movements

from the countryside to the major urban centres accelerated the pace of development in the capital.

However much Athens has tried to follow the model of modern big cities, it has never lost touch with the thread that links it to its long and exciting past.

14

The environs of the Acropolis

The Greek word *akropolis* is a compound formed from the words *akros* (topmost) and *polis* (city), and means literally the highest point of the city. Acropolises, that is fortified hills or crags, existed in many regions of Greece from prehistoric times. One such citadel was the Acropolis of Athens. In time, however, its role changed and it gradually became the most important cult centre of the city. By the mid-5th century BC it was home to some of the masterpieces of Classical architecture and sculpture.

The hill of the Acropolis, a steep crag only accessible from its west side, was first inhabited towards the end of the Neolithic Age. It was later transformed into a cult centre. View of the Acropolis from the west. In the foreground the Propylaia and the temple of Athena Nike, to the left the Erechtheion and to the right the Parthenon.

THE ACROPOLIS

Detail of a bronze statue of Athena, possibly by the sculptor Euphranor, c. 350 BC. Piraeus, Archaeological Museum.

The Acropolis was linked with the worship of Athena, goddess of wisdom, from as early as the Mycenaean period. Athena was the daughter of Zeus, king of gods and men, and Metis, goddess of prudence. While Metis was pregnant with Athena, Zeus received an oracle that she would first give birth to a daughter and afterwards to a son who would seize power. In order to defy the oracle Zeus swallowed Metis. Despite his precautions, when the time came for Athena's birth she emerged in panoply from her father's head. Athena quarrelled with Poseidon, god of the sea, for the protection of Athens, then called Kekropia after one of its autochthonous kings. In the end they decided that the city would be assigned to whoever offered it the greater gift, as adjudicated by the other gods. The contest took place on the rock of the Acropolis. Poseidon struck the ground with his trident and salt water gushed forth, while in a single movement Athena planted the world's first olive tree. The gods decided right away that Zeus' daughter was the victor and henceforth the city was known as Athens in her honour.

During the Archaic period several temples were built on the Acropolis, among them the Old Temple (*archaios naos*) of Athena and the temple referred to as the Hekatompedon, because it was 100 Attic feet long. From that time the sacred rock was a busy place. Alongside the temples, with their colourful painted pediments, stood smaller sacred edifices and countless *ex-votos*, that is offerings dedicated by the faithful to their beloved goddess. The Archaic Acropolis was set on fire by the Persians in 480 BC. After the war the Athenians gathered up the statues and architectural sculptures from the destroyed temples and buried them in pits in the rock. There they remained in oblivion until they were brought to light in excavations conducted between 1885 and 1891.

Some thirty years after the Persian invasion, Pericles, in his desire to make Athens the most splendid city in

1. Propylaia
2. Temple of Athena Nike
3. Parthenon
4. Erechtheion
5. Sancturay of Artemis Brauronia
6. Chalkotheke
7. Temple of Roma and Augustus
8. Sanctuary of Zeus Polieus
9. Pandroseion
10. Arrephorion

J. TRAVLOS
1967

Greece, implemented a well-organized and considered building plan. This included major projects on the Acropolis. According to later sources, Pheidias, a gifted sculptor and personal friend of Pericles, was appointed as its supervisor. He assembled a team of the most accomplished and imaginative architects and craftsmen of the day, who within a few years designed and constructed buildings of unsurpassed size and grace. Pericles, the visionary of a powerful and democratic Athens filled with magnificent buildings, died in the terrible plague that struck the city in 429 BC, but the programme he had initiated on the Acropolis continued after his death.

The Propylaia

The monumental entrance to the Acropolis was built on the west side of the rock on the site of the earlier and simpler propylon or gateway. Building began in 438 BC but was interrupted in 432 BC on the outbreak of the Peloponnesian War. Although the original plan was never completed, the Propylaia constructed under Pericles are a worthy complement to the Parthenon. The architect Mnesikles confronted the problems of limited space and steep incline of the ground in an ingenious manner. His creation, majestic and harmonious, represents an ideal introduction to the architectural forms inside the Acropolis.

The Propylaia complex comprises a central building flanked by two wings, a northwest and a southwest. On the façade of the central building stand six Doric columns, equidistant from each other, with the exception of the middle two which are wider apart in order to facilitate the entry of the horsemen and the animals in the Panathenaic procession. Two colonnades, each with three slender Ionic columns, were constructed perpendicular to the façade. The back part of the central building is at a higher level than the front. This difference in height between the two spaces, which communicated through five portals, was dealt with by using different roofs, the ceilings of which were painted deep blue and decorated with gold stars. The back face of the central building had six Doric columns, like the front.

The northwest wing of the Propylaia included the area known as the Pinakotheke, where visitors could relax, as the 2nd-century AD traveller Pausanias relates, and admire pictures painted on wooden panels. Among them were works by the famous 5th-century BC painter Polygnotos from Thasos. In front of the Pinakotheke stands the very high pedestal of 178 BC, on which a quadriga (four-horse chariot) had been set in honour of King Eumenes II of Pergamon. Later, in 15 BC, the same monument was dedicated to a Roman benefactor of Athens, Marcus Vipsanius Agrippa. Close to the second wing of the Propylaia, the southwest, a section of the Mycenaean wall of the Acropolis is visible. Lower down, in front of the Propylaia, is the Beulé gate. This was built after the sacking of Athens by the Herulians in AD 267 and is named after the French archaeologist who excavated it in the mid-19th century.

The temple of Athena Nike
To the southwest of the Propylaia, atop a Mycenaean defensive tower that was renovated in the Classical period, stands the temple of Athena Nike, in which Athena was worshipped with the epithet Nike (Victory).

The north side of the Propylaia. In the Ottoman period this space was used as a gunpowder store. In 1648 it was struck by lightning, causing an explosion that destroyed a large part of the Propylaia.

Nike (Wingless Victory) because the cult statue inside it was without wings. According to him, the Athenians had represented the goddess thus so that she would not fly away from their city.

The Parthenon

The multifaceted personality of the goddess Athena earned her numerous prosonyms, such as Nike (the victor), Ergane (she who taught men the crafts) Promachos (she who protected in battle). Sometimes she was simply referred to as Parthena (the virgin), for whom the great temple known as the Parthenon was erected on the Acropolis in the 5th century BC. Designed by the architects Iktinos and Kallikrates, its sculpted decoration was largely the creation of Pheidias. These great creators lived in a city brimful of new intellectual currents: they cast off the shackles of tradition, yet did not ignore them, and proceeded in innovative directions. Thus, through the amalgamation of familiar architectural elements from the Doric and Ionic orders, a new form emerged that could be dubbed Attic. The Parthenon, like the other artistic creations of the 5th century BC, expressed in its own language the new intellectual clime of the age. The clime that led to the birth of Tragedy and of Democracy.

The speed with which the Parthenon was built is remarkable indeed. Work commenced in 447 BC and the inauguration took place in 438 BC, even though the sculptures on the pediments were not completed until six years later, in 432 BC. It is all the more remarkable considering that this is the largest Doric temple in the ancient Greek world. It is the only one

The temple of Athena Nike. According to one myth, Theseus' father, Aegeus, committed suicide from here, because he thought his son had been killed by the Minotaur.

This elegant little amphiprostyle edifice has four columns in front and back. It was designed by the architect Kallikrates in 449 BC but completed much later, in 421 BC. Its frieze, almost all of which is in the British Museum, constitutes an important innovation. Instead of the usual mythical scenes an actual event is represented, the battle between the Greeks and the Persians at Plataeae. Around the temple was a parapet of marble plaques decorated on the external face with relief Nikai (Victories). Pausanias, erroneously believing that the monument was dedicated to the winged goddess Nike, refers to it as a temple of the Apteros

Wonderful depiction of the little Ionic temple of Athena Nike or of Nike Apteros (Wingless Victory), as it was called in Roman times. Watercolour by C.F. Werner, 1877. Athens, Benaki Museum.

Reconstruction of the southeast side of the Parthenon, giving an idea of the colours used on the sculpted decoration.

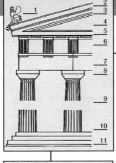

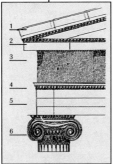

built almost entirely of marble. The only one with relief representations on all the metopes. However, its uniqueness is not just revealed by its size or its wealth of decoration – both the result of the city's prosperity –, it is revealed primarily by the details or refinements that transformed the lifeless blocks of marble into a single body pulsating with life.

The building's dimensions were determined by the ratio 4:9. This was the basis of the relationship of the diameter of the columns to the intercolumniations (the spaces between the axes of two successive columns), the height of the temple to its width, the width of the temple proper to its length. However, the strict symmetry did not produce a heavy, static construction, because vertical elements such as the columns and walls inclined slightly inwards externally. So the temple became pyramidal in shape, acquiring an upwards movement. In addition to the inclinations, some 'optical refinements', the curvatures and entaseis, were also applied in the Parthenon. For example, the stylobate, the surface on which the columns stand, is not absolutely horizontal but curves slightly in the middle. The columns also display entasis, a slight swelling at about 1/3 of their height. All these refinements not only endow the monument with a movement and vitality but also attest to the incredible precision with which it was constructed. It is sufficient to consider that in order to conform to the slopes and curvatures, each stone has its own specific shape and particular place in the whole.

The exterior of the Parthenon has columns on all four sides, 8 on the narrow ones and 17 on the long. The

Since the Archaic period the Athenians stamped Athena on the obverse of their coins and her sacred bird, the owl, on the reverse. In this particular representation the engraver copied the head of the ivory-and-gold statue of the goddess in the Parthenon. Silver tetradrachm of Athens, 129-128 BC. Athens, Numismatic Museum.

temple proper is hexastyle amphi-prostyle, that is with six columns in front and back. It is divided into two unequal parts, in the smaller of which, the west, are four Ionic columns to support the roof. Here, as in other parts of the temple, precious objects and state monies were kept. In the larger, east section, in front of a Π–shaped Doric colonnade, stood one of the seven wonders of the ancient world, the cult statue of Athena sculpted by Pheidias. The enormous chrys-elephantine statue, some 12 metres tall, stood upon a pedestal and represented the goddess standing and armed, with her left hand resting on her shield and her right holding a Nike.

The picture of the temple was completed by its sculpted decoration, born of Pheidias' fertile imagination and his pupils' consummate craftsmanship. In order to appreciate the vivid beauty of these works it should be kept in mind that the ancient Greeks enlivened their architectural sculptures and their statues with bright colours, mainly red, blue and gold. Many of the sculptures from the Parthenon, as well as from other monuments on the sacred rock, are exhibited in the Acropolis Museum. The majority however were sold by the Ottoman Turks to the British nobleman Lord Elgin, in the early 19th century, and were transported to the British Museum, where they remain to this day.

Placed above the colonnade surrounding the temple proper were 92 metopes, all decorated with reliefs. Represented on the east side was the Gigantomachy – the struggle between gods and giants –, on the west the Amazonomachy – the battle between Greeks and Amazons –, on the south the Centauromachy – the clash between the Lapiths of Thessaly and the Centaurs –, and on the north the Fall of Troy. The subjects of the metopes, inspired by the world of mythology, symbolize the overcoming of the forces of evil by the powers of good.

Pheidias' vision was not confined to

traditional mythological scenes however. Alongside these he wanted to laud the Athenian Democracy and, by extension, peaceful creation. So, contrary to established practice, he decided to transfer a vital and familiar image to marble; the people of Athens participating in one of their most joyous celebrations, the Pan-athenaic procession.

The Panathenaia, the major festival in honour of Athena, was held annually. Every four years however it was especially glorious, for which reason it was called the Great Panathenaia. On this occasion games and music competitions were organized. The most sacred part of the festival was the official procession which started from the Kerameikos and made its way to the Acropolis, bearing offerings to the goddess, primarily the sacred peplos, hung from the mast of a ship on wheels. With this peplos, woven by Athenian maidens, the priests clothed the ancient wooden effigy of Athena, the *xoanon*, which was believed to have fallen from heaven (*diipetes*). In order to present the Panathenaic procession, Pheidias resorted to a radical solution. He added an Ionic feature, the frieze, to the Doric building, placing it above the colonnades on front and back and high on the walls of the temple proper. On it he carved young horsemen, hoplites, old men, lyre-players (citharodes) and flute-players, young men and women with pitchers full of water, others leading animals for sacrifice or holding panniers of sweet-meats, maidens (*korai*) and masters of ceremonies (*teletarchai*). The lively, proud procession terminated at the east part of the frieze, where the seated Olympian gods all received the

The Erechtheion from the southwest, as depicted in the 19th-century.

sacrifices intended for Athena. The cycle of the decoration of the Parthenon was completed by the huge compositions on the pediments, unrivalled in conception and execution. The west presented the dispute between Athena and Poseidon for guardianship of the city, while the east the Birth of Athena from the head of Zeus. This scene had a special symbolic content for the Athenians, because the goddess's birth represented, as it were, the divine hypostasis of their city and the dawn of a new era for it.

The Erechtheion

The complex building to the north of the Parthenon, which once housed the *diipetes xoanon* (heaven-sent wooden effigy) of Athena as well as many age-old cults of Attica, is known as the Erechtheion. It owes its name to Erechtheus, the mythical king of Athens who in time seems to have been identified with Poseidon. The

Erechtheion was dedicated to Athena Polias, patron goddess of the city, and Poseidon-Erechtheus. It also enclosed the altars of Zeus Hypatos, Poseidon and Erechtheus, the hero Boutes (Erechtheus' brother) and Hephaistos, as well as the tomb of King Kekrops and the place where salt water gushed forth when Poseidon struck the rock with his trident. The sacred olive tree, Athena's gift to the city, sprouted to the west of the Erechtheion. Building of the temple began in 421 BC and it was completed in 405 BC. Its architect remains unknown, although some scholars suggest that it was Mnesikles. Whoever he was, he was presented with the formidable task of accommodating so many diverse elements of cult in one space, while taking into account the difficult configuration of the ground. The result was one of the most singular religious buildings in Antiquity. The Erechtheion comprises a main building to which two lateral structures were added, the

27

north porch and the porch of the Korai or Karyatides. It was built on four different levels and had three different roofs, Ionic columns of three different dimensions and, moreover, in accordance with an old Ionic custom, statues of Korai functioning as columns. These are the famous Karyatides, which tradition relates were named thus because they were as beautiful as the women from the Laconian city of Karyes.

Other sacred places

In Antiquity the Acropolis was filled with edifices, most of which have not survived. A sanctuary of Artemis Brauronia is known to have existed on the south side of the rock, near the Propylaia, and its founding was attributed to the tyrant Peisistratos, who hailed from Brauron. Next to it stood the building known as the Chalkotheke, in which – as its name implies – bronze (Gr. *chalkos*) vessels and precious *ex-votos* were stored. In the area now occupied by the Acropolis Museum lay a

sanctuary of Pandion, a mythical king of Athens, while discernible in front of the museum are the foundations of a circular Ionic temple of 27 BC, dedicated to the goddess Roma and the Roman Emperor Augustus.

To the northeast of the Parthenon there is evidence of the existence of a sanctuary of Zeus Polieus. On the north

side of the Acropolis, exactly in front of the Erechtheion, was the Pandroseion, where Pandrosos, one of Kekrops' three daughters, was worshipped. Another building, the Arrephorion, the dwelling of the Arrephorai, young girls who took part in mystical rites, stood further west. The picture of the Acropolis was completed by the altar to Athena and a host of votive offerings, outstanding among which was the colossal bronze statue of Athena Promachos, another work by Pheidias.

There were places of worship on the precipitous slopes of the crag as well, On the north, below the Pinakotheke, are remains of the Klepshydra, the most important fountain on the Acropolis and a source of potable water for the inhabitants of the area since Neolithic times. In the vicinity were three sanctuaries: of Apollo Hypoakraios, of Olympian Zeus and of Pan, the goat-footed god whom the Athenians believed had come to their aid in the Battle of Marathon. A little beyond was the sanctuary of Aphrodite and her son Eros. Last, it is suspected that Erse, another daughter of mythical Kekrops, was worshipped in a cave on the same slope, while her sister Agraulos was worshipped in caves on the east slope.

ACROPOLIS
USEFUL INFORMATION
Opening hours
Winter: daily 08.30-14.30
Summer: daily 08.30-18.30
Telephone: 32 14 172

THE ACROPOLIS MUSEUM

Built in 1874 in a hollow in the rock, so as not to mar the vista of the archaeological site, the Museum houses a unique collection of sculptures from the Acropolis excavations. These fall into two basic categories: architectural sculptures, which originally decorated buildings, and dedications to the goddess by devotees, the so-called *ex-votos*.

The exhibits span a large part of the Archaic period (600- 500/490 BC), the period of the Severe Style (500/490-460/450 BC) and the Classical period (450-323 BC). Outstanding among the Archaic works are the Korai, statues of young girls dedicated to Athena.

Clad in brightly coloured garments and with elaborate hairstyles, their principal feature is the famous Archaic smile, sometimes enigmatic and other-worldly, sometimes friendly and cheerful, which is encountered in all sculptures of the 6th century BC.

The Moschophoros, an exquisite Attic creation of around 570 BC. It represents a youth carrying a young calf on his shoulders, in order to offer it to the goddess Athena. The work is no longer the colossal size of the earlier Archaic statues and its face, with its friendly smile, is radiant with joy.

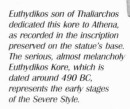

Euthydikos son of Thaliarchos dedicated this kore to Athena, as recorded in the inscription preserved on the statue's base. The serious, almost melancholy Euthydikos Kore, which is dated around 490 BC, represents the early stages of the Severe Style.

Excellent too are the works in the Severe Style, the transitional stage between Archaic and Classical art. The statues lost the monolithic rigidity of the Archaic ones and acquired movement by placing the weight of the body on one leg, usually the left. Concurrently the Archaic smile disappeared and the faces were suffused with an expression of introspection and reflection. Last, the Classical period, a period of maturity, is represented by some of the culminating achievements of ancient Greek art.

Vestibule
Exhibited in the entrance to the Museum are sculptures of different periods, among them a head of Alexander the Great (c. 330 BC), the statue of Prokne, daughter of Pandion, a work attributed to Pheidias' pupil Alkamenes (c. 430 BC), and the head of a philosopher (5th century AD).

Gallery I
Among the imposing architectural sculptures of the Archaic period, two works can be singled out. The pediment with Herakles exterminating the Lernaean Hydra and the massive poros pediment with the powerful representation of a lioness rending a calf.

The 'Pensive Athena', a votive relief of around 470 BC. The goddess, clad in Doric peplos and Corinthian helmet, leans on her spear, her head bowed in contemplation. No satisfactory explanation has yet been given of the rectangular stele in front of her. Perhaps it is a boundary stone (horos), marking her sanctuary.

Composition of three bearded male figures with a common body consisting of serpents' tails, known as the Three-bodied Daemon. The prevailing view today is that this is a representation of Nereus, the sea-monster with the ability to change its form. Section of the pediment of an Archaic temple on the Acropolis, 560-550 BC.

Gallery II
Pediments and *ex-votos* of the second half of the 6th century BC are the main exhibits here. Of particular interest are two poros groups: Herakles struggling with the sea daemon Triton and the three bearded men with serpentine body from the waist downwards. In a conspicuous position is the strikingly vital, smiling Moschophoros (Calf-bearer), dedicated by the Athenian aristocrat Rhombos. At the back of the gallery is the enigmatic poros pediment of 'Elia' or 'Troilus'.

Gallery III
The room is dominated by a representation of lions devouring a bull, which once adorned the central section of a pediment. Korai from island workshops are also displayed.

Gallery IV

This is dedicated to sculpture from the second half of the 6th century BC. Among the most important pieces is the famous 'Rampin' horseman, work of an anonymous artist, the wonderful hunting dog, the 'Persian' horseman and the Athena sculpted by Endoios. The greater part of the room is given over to the Acropolis Korai. The petite 'Peplophoros', thus named because she wears a simple Doric peplos, the charming 'Chian Kore', which was probably sculpted in an island workshop, and many others.

Gallery V

Prominent here are the figures from a pediment with a scene of the Gigantomachy, which are dated to the last quarter of the 6th century BC. Only three Giants and the impetuous Athena, who valiantly attacks her enemies, have survived. Beside them stands a dignified Kore, a work by the renowned sculptor Antenor.

Gallery VI

Gathered here are some of the masterpieces in the Severe Style. The 'Kritias Boy', the 'Blond Youth', whose hair was once coloured yellow, the

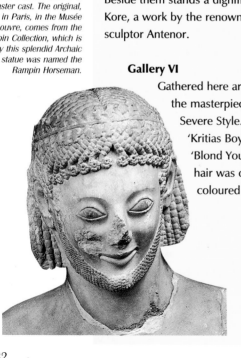

Front and side view of an exceptional example of the Severe Style: the 'Blond Youth'. It dates to the decade 490-480 BC and is considered to be a work by the sculptor Hegias, mentor of Pheidias.

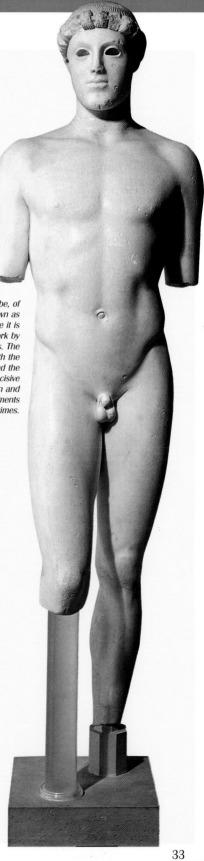

Statue of an ephebe, of 490-480 BC, known as the 'Kritias Boy', since it is suspected to be a work by the sculptor Kritias. The pose of the body, with the left leg stretched and the right relaxed is a decisive break with tradition and heralds the achievements of art in Classical times.

votive relief of the Pensive Athena, the Propylaia Kore and the serious Euthydikos Kore, thus named after its dedicator.

Gallery VII

A small room with sculptures from the decoration of the Parthenon. Among them are a metope from the south side of the temple, which shows a Centaur seizing a Lapith woman, and parts of the pediments: the group of Kekrops, the torso of Poseidon and the river Ilissos personified, from the west pediment; the torso of Hephaistos and the body of Selene, from the east.

Impressive marble dog of 530 BC. Another work by the creator of the Rampin Horseman.

Three plaques from the frieze on west side of the Parthenon, show young horsemen, participants in Panathenaic procession. On the f plaque the riders are ready to st. while on the other two they r impetuously, mounted bareback their stee

Gallery VIII

The gallery of the Parthenon frieze. The loveliest figures are of Poseidon, Apollo and Artemis, seated one behind the other in Olympian majesty, the dynamic horsemen, the youths leading oxen and the *hydriaphoroi* bearing pitchers full of water. In the same room are some figures from the Erechtheion frieze and reliefs from the parapet of the temple of Athena Nike, outstanding among which is the alluring Nike loosening her sandal.

Gallery IX

The visit to the Acropolis Museum ends with the image of four of the six Karyatides from the Erechtheion,

which were removed from the monument in order to protect them from atmospheric pollution, and replaced by copies. Of the other two, one has been destroyed and the other is in the British Museum.

Opposite the Karyatides is part of the 'Lenormant' relief, with the representation of a trireme.

The Parthenon frieze, a work of the period 442-438 BC, is one of the most ambitious expressions of Classical sculpture. On this plaque, which is from the frieze on the east side of the temple, three of the Olympian gods, Poseidon, Apollo and Artemis, watch the Panathenaic procession. Apollo turns behind to converse with Poseidon, while his sister Artemis looks straight ahead.

ACROPOLIS MUSEUM
USEFUL INFORMATION
Opening hours
Winter: daily 08.30-14.30
Summer: daily 08.00-18.30
Telephone: 32 35 665, 32 10 219

Aristophanes, the greatest comic poet of Antiquity, boldly tackled and lampooned current affairs from the viewpoint of the Athenian man in the street. Bust of Aristophanes, Roman copy of a 4th-century BC original. Paris, Musée du Louvre.

Euripides, playwright of such masterpieces as Medea, Electra, Orestes, Iphigenia in Aulis, Bacchants. Bust of Euripides, Roman copy of a 4th-century BC original. Naples, Museo Archeologico Nazionale.

THE SOUTH SLOPE OF THE ACROPOLIS

From the 5th century BC the south slope of the Acropolis was an important centre in the cultural life of Athens. Citizens attended music competitions in the Odeion of Pericles, while a little beyond, in the Theatre of Dionysos, the sufferings of Oedipus, Medea, Orestes and the heroes of ancient Greek Tragedy, were enacted.

There has been much discussion about the birth and development of ancient drama. The prevailing view is that its roots should be sought in the dithyramb, the improvised hymn that devotees sang while dancing in honour of the god Dionysos. Gradually, with the introduction of new elements, the dithyramb evolved into the first true theatrical manifestation in the Western world: ancient Greek drama. The three dramatic genres – tragic, satyrical and comic – were perfected in Athens in the 5th century BC.

The tragedies by Aeschylus, Sophocles and Euripides, as well as the comedies by Aristophanes remain to this day living monuments of an art non pareil. Throughout the 5th and most of the 4th century BC drama events were

Vase-paintings often shed light on interesting facets of everyday life in Antiquity. One of these is the theatre. Here, two actors are shown in their masks and costumes, after the end of a performance. Detail from the Pronomos krater, late 5th century BC. Naples, Museo Archeologico Nazionale.

organized primarily during the Great Dionysia, the splendid annual festival in honour of Dionysos. These events were in the form of competitions in which three dramatists participated after a selection process. Their plays were adjudicated by a committee of ten Athenians, which in the end declared the winner.

For the ancient Athenians the drama contests were one of the city's most important institutions, an inexhaustible source of intellectual instruction. Everyone attended, rich and poor, since from early on the state reimbursed indigent citizens with the cost of the ticket. The state also appointed the sponsors (choregoi), wealthy Athenians who defrayed the expenses of each performance.

Theatre of Dionysos

Like all ancient theatres it comprises three basic parts. The orchestra, a flat circular space in which the action took place, the skene, an elongated building

Aerial photograph of the Odeion of Herodes Atticus. The skene was originally decorated with mosaic pavements, statues and polychrome marble on the walls.

in which the actors changed costumes and which usually served as a backdrop too, and the cavea or auditorium, an amphitheatrical slope with tiered seats where the spectators sat. However, the Theatre of Dionysos did not always have the form that has survived to this day. Originally it was a wooden construction. Around the middle of the 4th century BC it was rebuilt on the initiative of the orator Lykourgos and the wooden tiers were replaced by marble seats. Later, during the Roman Age, various alterations and additions were made to the building, such as the paving of the orchestra with marble flags in the 1st century AD.

In the upper part of the Theatre of Dionysos remnants of the choregic monument of Thrasyllos (320-310 BC) can be seen, as well as the chapel of the Virgin Spiliotissa.

Sanctuary of Dionysos

The Theatre of Dionysos was part of the Sanctuary of Dionysos Eleuthereos, which began to take shape in the 6th century BC. The

The Odeion of Herodes Atticus was destroyed along with most of the buildings on the south slope of the Acropolis, by the Herulians in AD 267. It was restored during the 1960s.

remains of two temples have survived, the earlier one dated to the 6th century BC and the later to the 4th century BC.

Odeion of Pericles

At one time a huge square building with internal colonnades and a pyramidal roof stood to the east of the theatre. This was the Odeion of Pericles, erected during the years of his rule, the first roofed building in Athens in which music competitions were held. The Odeion of Pericles was burnt down in the 1st century BC. It was rebuilt not long after and continued to be used until it was razed to the ground by the Herulians. Its site is now occupied in part by the chapel of St George the Alexandrian, which was built to replace a 12th-century church that was destroyed in 1826.

Asklepieion

The cult of the healing god Asklepios was introduced to Athens towards the end of the 5th century BC. At that time an Asklepieion, a sanctuary of the god, was founded on the west side of the Theatre of Dionysos. The sick flocked there in search of a cure.

Summer performance in the Herodeion, as the Odeion of Herodes Atticus is popularly known to Athenians. It has a capacity of between 5000 and 6000 spectators.

Much later, in the 6th century AD, a basilica dedicated to the Christian physician-saints, the Sts Anargyroi, was built on the ruins of the Asklepieion.

'Street of the Tripods' - Choregic Monuments

The lower edge of the Asklepieion was skirted by the Peripatos, the road around the rock of the Acropolis. Two streets led into it: the Panathenaic Way and the Street of the Tripods, which began from the Prytaneion and reached as far as the Theatre of Dionysos. As its name indicates, the street was lined with the tripods offered by the deme of Athens to the sponsors (*choregoi*) of prize-winning plays and set up by them as *ex-votos*. These tripods were frequently incorporated in larger monuments, some of which still stand.

THEATRE OF DIONYSOS

USEFUL INFORMATION

Opening hours
Winter: daily 08.30-14.30
Summer: daily 08.30-18.30
Telephone: 32 24 625

Stoa of Eumenes

King Eumenes II of Pergamon built an enormous stoa below the Peripatos (197-159 BC). The Athenians congregated here during the intervals in theatrical performances, as well as for discussing when the weather prevented them from remaining outdoors.

Odeion of Herodes Atticus

The most impressive monument on the south slope of the Acropolis is the Odeion built between AD 167 and 174 by Herodes Atticus, in memory of his wife Regilla. According to ancient testimonies this was a very luxurious building with a wonderful roof of cedar wood. Today the Odeion has lost much of its former splendid aspect, but nevertheless is still a superb venue for theatrical, musical and other events. After so many centuries Herodes Atticus continues to contribute to the cultural enhancement of his beloved city.

Agamemnon, leader of the Trojan campaign, was murdered by his wife Clytemnestra and her paramour Aegisthos. Eight years later Agamemnon's son, Orestes, took his revenge. In this representation Orestes kills his mother, thrusting his sword into her body. Aegisthos, right, runs to seek protection at the altar, looking backwards in fear. Bronze strip, c. 570 BC. Olympia, Archaeological Museum.

THE AREOPAGOS

A short distance to the northwest of the Acropolis is the rocky hill of the Areopagos. Myth has it that on this rock (*pagos*) Ares, god of war, was tried for the murder of one of the sons of Poseidon. Also, as Aeschylus narrates in the *Orestian Trilogy*, Orestes, son of Agamemnon, was tried on the Areopagos for the murder of his mother Clytemnestra.

The hill of the Areopagos was the seat of the homonymous executive and judiciary body, which was made up mainly of members of the aristocracy. Prior to the Classical period the Areopagos had enormous influence on the political life of Athens. However, in the reforms of Ephialtes it lost most of its powers, retaining only the right to try premeditated murder and some other sacriligeous crimes.

The last important event in the history of the Areopagos is associated with Christianity. The

Ares, the harsh and relentless god of war, was once tried for murder on a rock in Athens, which has been known as the Areopagos ever since. A depiction of Ares from a black- figure krater of around 570 BC, known as the 'François Vase'. Florence, Museo Archeologico.

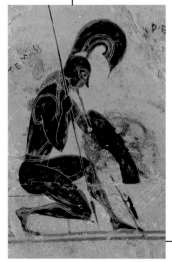

Apostle Paul is said to have preached to the Athenians here, in AD 51, on the existence of a new, hitherto unknown god. The first Athenian to be baptized a Christian was Dionysios the Areopagite, now the patron saint of Athens.

THE HILL OF THE NYMPHS

To the west of the Acropolis rises the hill of the Nymphs, which is topped by the National Observatory. This Neoclassical building was designed by two foreign architects, the Dane Hansen and the German Schaubert, and erected between 1840 and 1846.

THE PNYX

The Pnyx, one of the places where the Ekklesia of the deme assembled, is also close to the Acropolis. From the time of Pericles onwards all Athenian citizens participated in the Ekklesia. They voted in new laws, elected many of the archons and monitored the management of the city's finances. The Athenians were the masters of their fate. Thousands of them gathered here forty times a year, in order to decide on all matters concerning the city. The steps of the bema or dais from which the speakers addressed the assemblies of the deme of Athens still exist.

THE **HILL** OF **PHILOPAPPOS**

The hill to the southwest of the Acropolis was known in Antiquity as Mouseion, either because the tomb of the poet Mousaios was located here or, more likely, because there was a sanctuary (*temenos*) of the Muses. On its summit are the foundations of a fortified enceinte built in 294 BC by the King of Macedon, Demetrios Poliorcetes. Later, between AD 114 and 116, the funerary monument of Gaius Julius, Antiochus Philopappos was erected on the same spot. The consul's portrait statue can still be seen in one of the niches on the monument, while beside it is the statue of his grandfather, Antiochus IV, King of Commagene. Many

centuries later, in 1687, the Venetian general Morosini chose this site as an emplacement for the cannon with which he bombarded the Acropolis. Today many Athenians climb up Philopappos hill on Shrove Monday (*Kathari Deftera*), when it is customary to fly colourful paper kites.

▶
The monument of Philopappos, grandson of the King of Commagene. When the kingdom was dissolved by the Romans in AD 72, Philopappos sought refuge in Athens. In recognition of his benefactions to the city he was granted the rights of an Athenian citizen as well as permission to build his monumental tomb in a conspicuous position, opposite the Acropolis.

The ancient monuments have always held a fascination for foreign visitors to Greece. The many depictions of them by European travellers of past centuries are nowadays an invaluable source of information on historical reality in those times. The Philopappos Monument. Watercolour by L.F. Cassas, c. 1795. Athens, Benaki Museum.

The Dormition of the Virgin. A notable work of the Costantinopolitian School, with balanced composition and muted colours. In the four corners, around the central representation, are scenes from the Life of the Virgin. Dated to the late 14th century.

THE **CANELLOPOULOS MUSEUM**

A Neoclassical mansion on the north slope of the Acropolis is now home to the Paul and Alexandra Canellopoulos Collection, which was donated to the Greek state in 1972. It includes a large number of antiquities and works of art which illustrate in their own special way the cultural course of Hellenism from prehistoric times to the present day.

Ground floor

Displayed in the first three rooms of the Museum are Byzantine and Venetian coins, Byzantine jewellery, bronze and clay vases and lamps, ecclesiastical vessels, crosses, chalices, Byzantine lead seals, Coptic textiles from Egypt and several icons dating from the 14th to the 18th century. Among the last are many signed works by distinguished painters, such as the Beheading of St (Paraskevi), by Michael Damaskenos (16th century), Christ, by Emmanuel Lambardos (17th century) and Archangel Michael, by the Hiermonk Iakovos (17th-18th century). Of particular

▶

Terracotta figurine of a chariot with warrior. Late Geometric period.

interest in the fourth room are the funerary portraits that were placed on mummies, unearthed at El Fayum in Egypt.

Lower mezzanine

Among the most important exhibits here are the Postbyzantine icons by Theodoros Poulakis and Emmanuel Tzanes (17th century), the Neohellenic folk jewellery (18th-19th century), the manuscripts and the wooden and clay stamps for loaves of blessed bread.

Basement

Displayed in these rooms are Postbyzantine and later icons, folk jewellery and various other objects such as cups, crosses and embroideries of different periods.

Courtyard

The majority of pieces here are funerary stelai and lekythoi of the Classical period.

Upper mezzanine

The two rooms here are dedicated to the dawn of Greek culture. The exhibits, mainly vases, figurines, weapons and jewellery, begin from the Neolithic Age (6000-2800/2700 BC), span the Early Cycladic (3200-2000 BC),

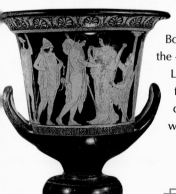

...rracotta figurine of the late ...h century BC, from a ...nagra workshop. A young ...rl, perhaps a Muse, sits ...d plays her lyre. She ...ars a blue ribbon ...th flowers in her red ...ir and her head is ...rned to the side with ...nostalgic air.

the Minoan (2800-1100 BC) and Mycenaean cultures (1600-1100 BC), down to Geometric times (900-700 BC). There are also a few works from the civilizations of the Near and the Middle East, as well as vases of coloured glass paste, known as Phoenician (6th-2nd century BC).

Part of a Corinthian alabastron, that is a vase for aromatic oils. Decorated with dancing figures and incised rosettes, it dates from the early 6th century BC.

First floor

Attic red-figure krater of 420 BC, work of the 'Dinos Painter'. On the front an armed youth bids farewell to his child, held in the arms of a young woman. Seated on the right is his white-haired father, while standing on the left are two other young men holding hunting equipment. The name 'Meleagros', faintly visible above the head of the first youth, indicates that the scene is inspired by the mythological hunt of the Calydonian Boar, in which the hero Meleagros distinguished himself.

In the vestibule of the first floor are gold jewellery of the Classical and Hellenistic periods, Roman jewellery and sculpture, as well as a few impressive pieces of Persian jewellery and *objets d'art* of the 5th and 6th centuries AD. In the other rooms are works of Archaic, Classical, Hellenistic and Roman times. Outstanding among them are the wonderful black-figure and red-figure Attic vases, and the 'Tanagraies', the graceful terracotta female figurines produced in the renowned coroplastic workshops of the Boeotian town of Tanagra in the 4th and 3rd centuries BC. Last, before leaving the first floor, the exquisite frescoes decorating the ceilings are well worth admiring.

CANELLOPOULOS MUSEUM

USEFUL INFORMATION

Opening hours
Tuesday-Sunday: 08.30-15.00 Closed Monday
Address: 12 Panos and Theorias St, Plaka
Telephone: 32 12 313

PLAKA

'Last night and the night before on the Acropolis: nights with full moon ... The little houses to the northeast, like a school of turtles in the age of cubism, with shell silken colour of crow feather or silver. The day before yesterday (after the rain) they shimmered in the moonlight like dolphin skin. Human among so much inhuman ...'

(G. Seferis, Days I, 28/5/1926)

Detail of a Neoclassical house in Plaka.

The heart of old Athens beats in the narrow streets of Plaka, the fascinating neighbourhood that spreads to the north and northeast of the Acropolis. The most plausible explanation of its name is that it derives from the Albanian word *pliakou*, which means old. It was described as *pliakou* by the Albanian soldiers who settled here during the Ottoman period, probably in the 16th century.

At the end of the Greek War of Independence Plaka was a heap of rubble. In no time, however, it began to recover and revive. New houses were built, some copying the earlier ones of Ottoman times and others in the Neoclassical order.

Over the years Plaka gradually lost its residential character. This change reached its peak in the 1960s, when it was mainly a tourist haunt and commercial quarter. Even so it managed to escape the building developments in the rest of Athens and to preserve its traditional aspect. Behind every corner hides the incomparable magic of old Athens.

Anaphiotika

At the foot of the north slope of the Acropolis a piece of the Cyclades has been transplanted harmoniously in Athens. Cycladic craftsmen came to the new capital to find work during the reign of King Otto, when there was a building boom. Most of them poor, they built humble homes, without planning permission, on the steep, rocky terrain, which so closely resembles their native islands. Thus a neighbourhood resembling a Cycladic village took shape. It is called Anaphiotika because most of the first inhabitants were migrants from Anaphi.

The Old University

Many of the houses in Plaka have a story to tell, like the one on Tholos street, high up in Ano Plaka. A very old building, perhaps pre-18th century, it

Typical alleyways in Plaka.

The charming old Athenian church of St Nicholas Rangava. Its bell was the first to toll after the liberation of Athens from the Germans, on 12 October 1944.

▶

The choregic monument of Lysikrates, which had been built alongside similar monuments in the ancient 'Street of the Tripods'.

was was bought in 1831 by the architects Kleanthis and Schaubert. A few years later, in 1837, it was chosen as the premises for the first University of Athens. From the mid-19th century onwards it changed hands several times and for a while was a taverna, named the 'Palaio Panepistimio' (Old University). Today it is a University Museum.

The churches

Crammed in and amongst the houses, in the narrow sreets of Plaka, are several Byzantine and Postbyzantine churches. One of the oldest is that of the Transfiguration of Christ (Metamorphosis tou Soteros) (1050-1150) in Theorias street, near the Canellopoulos Museum. Further up, in Anaphiotika, are the churches of St Symeon and St George of the Rock (17th century). On the way down the steps from Anaphiotika stands the church of St John the Theologian, with its original 12th-century masonry, and very close by, at the end of

Prytaneion street, is St Nicholas Rangava, a typical Byzantine church of the 11th-12th century, which was added to and repaired in 1977-78. Not far from here, beside Lysikrates Square, stands the church of St Catherine of the Sinai Monastery (11th-12th century), to which later interventions have also been made. Another well-known church in Plaka is the Saviour Kottakis (Soteira tou Kottaki) in Kydathenaion street, which was built in the 11th-12th century on the site of an earlier, 6th-century church.

Lysikrates Square

At the centre of this picturesque little square in the eastern corner of Plaka stands the choregic monument of Lysikrates, built in 335-334 BC and popularly known in later times as 'Diogenes' Lantern'. Represented on its frieze is the god Dionysos battling with pirates, a subject perhaps inspired by the theatrical work that brought distinction to its sponsor (*choregos*), Lysikrates. In the mid-17th century the monument was incorporated in the adjacent Capuchin monastery and transformed into a Catholic chapel. For many years this monastery provided accommodation for distinguished visitors, such as the British philhellene and poet, Lord Byron. During the Greek War of Independence the Capuchin Monastery was destroyed, but Lysikrates' monument, the only intact choregic monument in Athens, has survived to this day.

Embroidered scene of a wedding ceremony. Left, the bride between two companions, right, the groom on a blue horse. In front of him stands the bratimos or adelphopoitos, that is his bosom friend, who customarily played an important role in the elaborate nuptial celebrations in Epirus. Part of the border of a bridal sheet from Ioannina. Late 18th-early 19th century. Athens, Museum of Greek Folk Art.

Silver palaskes, pouches for gunpowder, with representations in savati, a kind of niello. On the one above is the figure of St George, while below is the personification of Freedom, holding a severed enemy head. Late 19th-early 20th century. Athens, Museum of Greek Folk Art.

THE MUSEUM OF GREEK FOLK ART

Greek folk art, with its expressive spontaneity and vitality, is the continuation of Byzantine, and by extension ancient Greek art. In parallel it has absorbed and assimilated diverse elements borrowed from West and East. Its creations, inextricably linked with the needs of everyday life and executed with great skill and unbounded imagination, are uniquely interesting. The museum in Kydathenaion street houses an impressive array of all manifestations of Greek folk art, from the period of its great heyday during the last 150 years of Ottoman rule, into modern times. On the ground floor are colourful embroideries, masterpieces from different regions of Greece. On the mezzanine floor are mainly ceramics, woodcarvings and metal vessels. Part of the same space is given over to figures of Karangiozis and other heroes of the folk shadow-puppet theatre, a peculiar genre of theatrical art that has its roots in the Far East. Here too are costumes worn as disguises in events that surely derive from the ancient Dionysiac festivals. The first floor is dedicated to Theophilos Hadjimichail, the great, self-taught, naïve painter who drew his inspiration from Greek history and mythology, folk tales and everyday life. Temporary exhibitions on different themes are also mounted here. On the second floor are works of silver-smithing, such as intricate jewellery,

weapons, gunpowder flasks and ecclesiastical vessels. On the top floor of the museum are many traditional regional costumes.

Head of a woodcarved distaff, used together with a spindle for spinning raw wool into thread. This exquisite tool was crafted in the late 19th-early 20th century. Athens, Museum of Greek Folk Art.

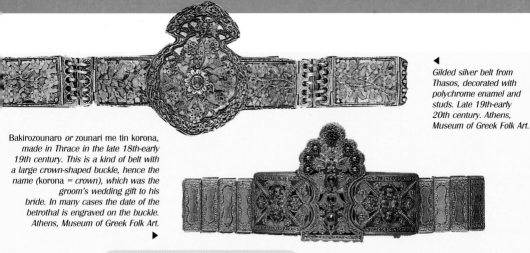

◄ Gilded silver belt from Thasos, decorated with polychrome enamel and studs. Late 19th-early 20th century. Athens, Museum of Greek Folk Art.

Bakirozounaro *or zounari me tin korona*, made in Thrace in the late 18th-early 19th century. This is a kind of belt with a large crown-shaped buckle, hence the name (korona = crown), which was the groom's wedding gift to his bride. In many cases the date of the betrothal is engraved on the buckle. Athens, Museum of Greek Folk Art.
▶

THE CENTRE OF FOLK ART AND TRADITION

Angeliki Hadjimichali, born in Plaka in 1895, literally worshipped Greek folk art and devoted herself to its study, leaving a significant body of scholarly work behind her. Her family home, in the street named after her, now houses a collection of works of Greek folk art, including woodcarvings and textiles, costumes, embroideries, clay vases and copper vessels, tools and raw materials for weaving, as well as personal effects of Angeliki Hadjimichali.

◄ Alexander the Great and his legendary campaigns hold a special place in the painting of Theophilos Hadjimichail. In this work Alexander is depicted as an archangel on horseback, brandishing a glaive. Mural by Theophilos, early 20th century. Athens, Museum of Greek Folk Art.

The adventures of Erotokritos and Arethusa, protagonists in one of the Medieval romances that circulated in popular editions in Greece, in the 19th century, was one of Theophilos Hadjimichail's favourite subjects. In this painting the two sweethearts are depicted on Arethusa's balcony, which Erotokritos has scaled with a rope ladder. Oil-painting by Theophilos, early 20th century. Athens, Museum of Greek Folk Art.

MUSEUM OF GREEK FOLK ART
USEFUL INFORMATION
Opening hours
Tuesday-Sunday: 10.00-14.00
Closed Monday
Address: 17 Kydathenaion St, Plaka
Telephone: 32 29 031

CENTRE OF FOLK ART AND TRADITION
USEFUL INFORMATION
Opening hours
Tuesday-Friday: 09.00-13.00, 17.00-21.00
Saturday-Sunday: 09.00-13.00 Closed Monday
Address: 6 A. Hadjimichali St, Plaka
Telephone: 32 43 987

Part of the hem of a woman's chemise from Crete, embroidered with vegetal and symbolic motifs, 18th century. Athens, Museum of Greek Folk Art.

THE MUSEUM OF GREEK FOLK MUSICAL INSTRUMENTS

In Diogenous street, close to the Roman Agora, is the mansion built by the freedom-fighter (*oplarchigos*) Georgios Lassanis in 1842. Here is exhibited part of the rich collection of musical instruments donated to the Greek state by the musicologist Phoivos Anoyiannakis. On the ground floor and the first floor are various types of traditional instruments, among them clarinets (*klarina*), bagpipes (*tsabounes*), shawms (*zournades*), *baglamades*, lyres and mandolins (*mandoles*). In the basement are peculiar instruments and sound-producing objects, such as bells, spoons, children's whistles, shells and wooden gongs (*semantra*). Next to each show-case are earphones for those who want to hear the sound, the technique of playing and the combination of the musical instruments on display.

The lovely building that houses the Museum of Greek Folk Musical Instruments.

MUSEUM OF GREEK FOLK MUSICAL INSTRUMENTS
USEFUL INFORMATION
Opening hours
Tuesday, Thursday-Sunday: 10.00-14.00
Wednesday: 12.00-18.00 Closed Monday
Address: 1 Diogenous St, Plaka
Telephone: 32 54 119

The Aerides Bath-House

The female members of a family at the bath-house. Illustration from the 19th-century volume Eski Istanbul 'da Gundelik Hayat, *which is in the 'Bosporis' Archive.*

The history of the hamam in Greece begins right after the country's conquest by the Ottomans. Modelled on the public baths of Roman and Byzantine times, the Ottoman hamams are linked with bodily hygiene, the cure of certain ailments and the cleansing of the soul. They also played a significant role in the social life of the period, especially for women, since they were meeting places and centres of leisure. Hamams were either twin, that is with separate facilities for men and women, or single, with common facilities used by men and by women separately at different hours of the day. As a rule they comprised three areas in axial arrangement: the changing rooms (places of reception, waiting as well as relaxation and amusement after the bath), the tepid chambers and the hot chambers. Three hamams are mentioned in Athens, in the first period of Ottoman rule. The only one still extant is the hamam of Abid Effendi, the so-called Aerides Bath-house, which operated until 1965. It was ceded to the Museum of Greek Folk Art in 1984 and a few years later work began on its restoration, which was completed in 1998. This unique monument for Athens will soon open as a museum devoted to bath-houses from antiquity to recent times.

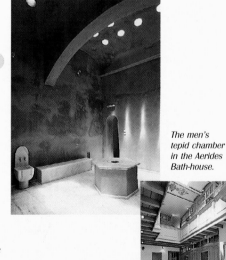

The men's tepid chamber in the Aerides Bath-house.

The women's changing rooms in the Aerides Bath-house.

The area of the Ancient Agora

Ancient Agora
Museum of the Ancient Agora
Roman Agora
Horologion of Andronikos Kyrrhestes
Library of Hadrian
Monastiraki
Metropolis
Panaghia Gorgoepikoos
Kapnikarea
Hagioi Asomatoi
Kerameikos
Kerameikos Museum

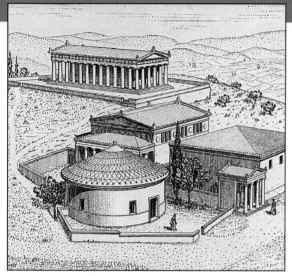

Restoration drawing of some of the buildings in the ancient Athenian Agora. In the foreground the Tholos, adjacent to it the Old and the New Bouleuterion, and in the background the temple of Hephaistos.

The sun has risen and the day is beinning in the Agora. Two vendors are laying out their wares on their stalls – fish from the Saronic gulf and fresh greens from the Mesogeia. People are crowding in front of the ballot boxes (*kleroteria*), to find out whether they've been drawn as judges in the Heliaia Lawcourt. Further off, a few men are commenting on the latest stormy assembly of the Ekklesia of the Deme. Others are arriving to make sacrifice at the altar of the Twelve Gods or, perhaps, in the temple of Apollo Patroos ... An ordinary day in the Agora, the busiest place in ancient Athens, was something like this.

THE ANCIENT AGORA

The history of the site of the ancient Agora goes back to prehistoric times. The area was initially a cemetery. With the political reforms in the 6th century BC, it was established as a centre of the city's political, religious and social life. So it began to fill gradually with public buildings, temples and altars, acquiring its final form in the 2nd century BC. In the following years the Agora was destroyed and plundered several times. Even so, new edifices were erected, particularly during the 2nd century AD. It was finally deserted after the Slav raids in AD 580, and remained desolate until the 10th century, when a settlement was founded here. The last inhabitants left in 1931, when the archaeologist's spade began to dig up from the depths of time the long-lost picture of the ancient Agora of Athens.

Marble bust of the Roman period. Some scholars believe it to be a copy of the bronze portrait statue of the great Athenian legislator Solon, which stood, according to Pausanias, in front of the Poikile (Painted) Stoa. Naples, Museo Archeologico Nazionale.

North Section.

Excavations on the north side of the Agora have brought to light traces of buildings of various periods. These include a basilica, that is a public building of the 2nd century AD, and the Stoa of the Herms, in which stood square-pillars topped with busts of the god Hermes, the herms. To the north of present Adrianou street stood the so-called Poikile or Painted Stoa (c. 470-460 BC), decorated, with famous paintings.

It was in the Poikile Stoa that the philosopher Zenon taught, in the 3rd century BC, which is why his followers were called Stoics.

Central section

At the north end of the central part of the Agora is the ruined altar of the Twelve Gods. The altar was built together with its enclosure (*peribolos*) in 522-521 BC, by Peisistratos the Younger, grandson and namesake of the tyrant. It was established as the starting point for measuring the distance between Athens and other cities. In front of the altar are the

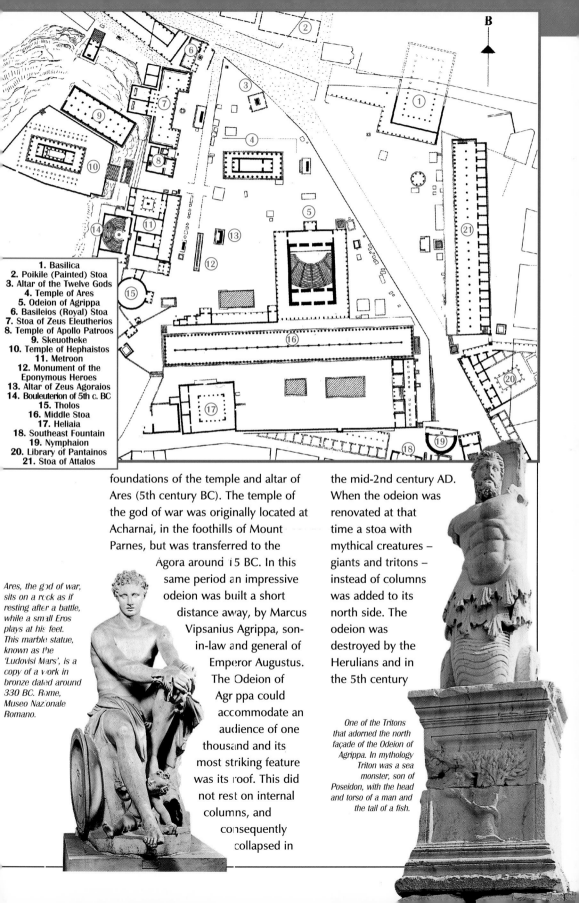

B

foundations of the temple and altar of Ares (5th century BC). The temple of the god of war was originally located at Acharnai, in the foothills of Mount Parnes, but was transferred to the Agora around i5 BC. In this same period an impressive odeion was built a short distance away, by Marcus Vipsanius Agrippa, son-in-law and general of Emperor Augustus. The Odeion of Agrippa could accommodate an audience of one thousand and its most striking feature was its roof. This did not rest on internal columns, and consequently collapsed in the mid-2nd century AD. When the odeion was renovated at that time a stoa with mythical creatures – giants and tritons – instead of columns was added to its north side. The odeion was destroyed by the Herulians and in the 5th century

Ares, the god of war, sits on a rock as if resting after a battle, while a small Eros plays at his feet. This marble statue, known as the 'Ludovisi Mars', is a copy of a work in bronze dated around 330 BC. Rome, Museo Nazionale Romano.

One of the Tritons that adorned the north façade of the Odeion of Agrippa. In mythology Triton was a sea monster, son of Poseidon, with the head and torso of a man and the tail of a fish.

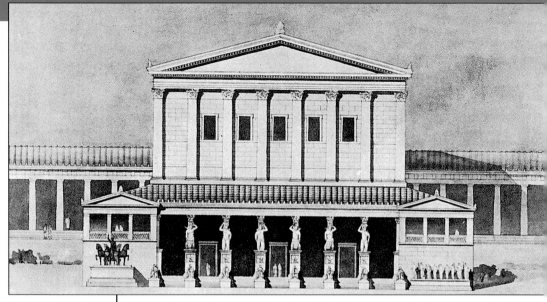

AD a new building was erected on its site. According to earlier scholars this was a gymnasium, a place for physical and mental exercise, while a more recent view is that it was an administrative building, possibly belonging to the brother of the famed Athenian empress of Byzantium, Athenaïs-Eudoxia.

West section

At the northwest edge of the Agora stood the Basileios or Royal Stoa, built in the late 6th century BC as seat of one of the nine archons of the city, the archon-basileus. The main responsibilities of this archon were, after the mid-5th century BC, to preside over the Areopagos and to supervise certain Athenian festivals. Wooden pillars on which the ancestral laws of the city were written were set up in the Basileios Stoa. It was here, in 399 BC, that Socrates was interrogated and sent for trial.

The Athenian philosopher, whom three fellow citizens accused of impiety to the gods and seducing young men, was sentenced to death by drinking the poison hemlock. In 430-420 BC the larger Stoa of Zeus Eleutherios was built alongside the Basileios Stoa, and in the 4th century BC the small Ionic temple of Apollo Patroos. Here Apollo was worshipped as founder of the Ionian tribe, to which the Athenians belonged.

Between these two buildings was the little temple of Zeus Phatrios and Athena Phatria (4th century BC), and not far behind was a large rectangular building (3rd century BC) which perhaps functioned as a Skeuotheke, where precious vessels were kept. Further north was a temenos (sacred precinct) of the Deme and the Graces (2nd century BC), and a small Hellenistic building, which some scholars have identified as the temple of Aphrodite Urania.

Atop the hill of Agoraios Kolonos stands a wonderfully well-preserved temple, the 'Hephaisteion', a Doric edifice dedicated to Hephaistos, patron deity of metal-workers and especially bronzesmiths. Athena Ergane, protectress of potters and craftsmen,

was also worshipped on the same spot, which is why the slopes of the hill were once full of potters', bronze-smiths' and blacksmiths' shops. Construction of the temple of Hephaistos started in the decade 460-450 BC and evidently finished before 420 BC. It is of peripteral type, i.e. surrounded by a colonnade, and its metopes bore relief scenes: those on the east side represent the Labours of Herakles, while the rest, as well as a section of the frieze, the Labours of Theseus. The predominant role of Theseus in the decoration of the temple explains why it was erroneously called the 'Theseion' until the mid-19th century. Inside the temple proper, two bronze cult statues stood on a single pedestal: one was of Athena and the other, by the renowned sculptor Alkamanes, was of

Hephaistos, son of Zeus and Hera, was born lame, so his ashamed mother flung him into the sea. When he grew up he forgave her, thanks to the intervention of Dionysos, god of wine, who made Hephaistos drunk in order to lead him back to Olympos. In the representation the drunken Hephaistos returns to Olympos, propped up by a Satyr, while Dionysos walks before him. Detail of a red-figure pelike. 435-430 BC. Munich, Staatliche Antikensammlungen.

Hephaistos. In the 5th century AD or slightly later the temple was converted into a church, dedicated to St George. It was here that mass was celebrated on 1 December 1834, welcoming King Otto to Athens.

On the visitor's right as he/she descends the Agoraios Kolonos are the ruins of the Metroon (2nd century BC). This building housed the public documents and civic lists of Athens, where citizens registered their children on the tenth day after birth. Since the 6th century BC a sanctuary of Ge existed here. The primeval goddess Ge seems to have been identified with her daughter Rhea, 'Mother of the Gods', who in turn was associated with Demeter, goddess of agriculture, as well as with an Oriental deity, the 'Great Mother'. Preserved in front of the Metroon are the ruins of an oblong dais (4th century BC) on which stood statues of the ten mythical heroes after whom the ten tribes of Athens were named. White-painted wooden 'notice boards' were hung on the front of the Monument of the Eponymous Heroes. Behind it was the altar of Zeus

View of the temple of Hephaistos. Like many other ancient monuments in Athens its walls and columns are covered with graffiti from Ottoman times, ranging from references to historical events to animals, birds, ships and names of foreign travellers. Lower down are the foundations of buildings in the Agora, from the Stoa of Zeus Eleutherios to the Metroon.

▶ Agoraios (4th century BC). Adjacent to the Metroon are the foundations of the old Bouleuterion. The headquarters of the Boule became defunct in the late 5th century BC, when the new Bouleuterion was built to the west of it. During the heyday of the Athenian Democracy, the Boule had 500 members whose term of office lasted one year. The Athenians, who were divided into ten tribes, voted annually to elect 100 citizens from each tribe, the *prokritoi*. From these candidates, 50 were selected by drawing lots. The 50 *bouleutai* (deputies) from each tribe then drew lots to appoint the *prytaneis* (presidents). In other words they formed a kind of government for a session equal to one tenth of a year. The *prytaneis* resided and dined in the Tholos (470-460 BC), the circular building next to the Bouleuterion. The standards for the city's weights and measures were also kept in the Tholos.

South section
As the visitor proceeds southeastwards from the Tholos, he/she passes the ruins of three stoas: the Middle Stoa (2nd century BC), the South Stoa I (5th century BC) and the South Stoa II (2nd century BC). The square building adjacent to South Stoa II was probably the seat of the Haliaia, the most important lawcourt in Classical Athens. Jurors were chosen by lot from the pool of 6000, 600 from each tribe of Athens. Various other installations stood further west, such as a fountain, a public water-clock in Classical times, and, just outside the bounds of the Agora, a building of the 5th century BC. In the opinion of some scholars this was the prison where Socrates spent his last days. The ruins of many private houses

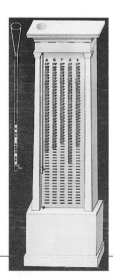
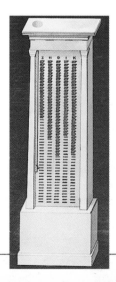

Section of the paved 'Panathenaic Way', which survives in quite good condition on the southeast side of the ancient Agora.

were revealed close to the hill of the Areopagos. Those dating to the Classical period were probably dwellings of artisans or tradesmen, while those of the 4th and 5th centuries AD belonged to Sophists. Tradition has it that the Sophists taught at home, where they also provided lodgings for their favourite pupils. Several other buildings have been excavated in the southeast corner of the Agora, around the beautiful 11th-century Byzantine church of the Hagioi Apostoloi (Holy Apostles) tou Solaki. The most notable of these are a fountain-house (second half of 6th century BC), most probably the Enneakrounos mentioned by Pausanias, the Athens Mint (5th century BC) and the Nymphaion (sanctuary of the Nymphs) (2nd century AD). Further south, a short distance from the rock of the Acropolis, one of the most

important and revered sanctuaries in the city was founded. This was the sanctuary of Demeter and her daughter Persephone (Kore), the famous Eleusinion *En Astei* (i.e. in the city).

East section

The greater part of the east side of the Agora is occupied by the restored Stoa of Attalos. Around AD 100 a large library was built by Titus Flavius Pantainos at its south end. In front of the Stoa are a bema (2nd century BC), a small circular building (2nd century AD) that housed the statue of some god, and a section of the 'Panathenaic Way', the road leading from the Dipylon, the main gate of the city, to the Acropolis.

View of the ancient Agora and the restored Stoa of Attalos.

▶ *The colonnades of the façade of the Stoa of Attalos.*

THE MUSEUM OF THE ANCIENT AGORA

Overlooking the east side of the Agora is the two-storey stoa donated to Athens by Attalos II, King of Pergamon (159-138 BC), as a token of his gratitude towards the city in which he had studied, that is his intellectual home. In antiquity the Stoa of Attalos was a shopping centre, with 21 shops on each floor. The restored building that exists today, an exact replica of the ancient one, houses very interesting finds from the area of the ancient Athenian Agora.

▶ *Terracotta votive plaque of the 7th century BC.*

Bronze protome of Nike.

Displayed on the ground-gloor, behind the columns of the internal colonnade, are statues of various periods. Some of the most important works are the Apollo Patroos, by the sculptor Euphranor (4th century BC), the Iliad and the Odyssey, sculptures that probably come from the Library of Pantainos (2nd century AD), the majestic statue thought to represent Aphrodite (early 4th century BC, a votive relief dedicated to the god Pan and the Nymphs (c. 330 BC) and another relief, commemorating the victory of the Leontis tribe in horse races (early 4th century BC).

On entering the museum the visitor sees artefacts of Neolithic and Mycenaean times. Presented next are *kterismata,* that is the grave goods that accompanied the dead, from the Geometric period. Also exhibited in this first section of the museum are the grave of a young girl (c. 100 BC), a burial pithos

Terracotta statuette of a young athlete. Dated around 540-530 BC.

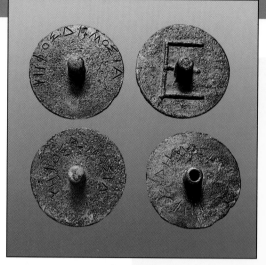

Four judgement psephoi (counters). The form of their axis determined the verdict. The solid axis meant acquittal, the hollow one condemnation. Each judge held the psephos between his thumb and index finger, in such a way that the axis was concealed, and placed it in the container. When all the psephoi had been gathered, they were then counted.

The length of time that the accused and the plaintiff were allowed to speak in the law court was determined according to the seriousness of the case and was measured by clepsydras, such as the one illustrated here. Clepsydras were made in various shapes, corresponding to different lengths of time, and were filled with water which flowed slowly from the top part through a small hole into the bottom.

with the bones of an infant and some impressive *kterismata* from a funerary pyre of around 725 BC. The finds in the central part of the museum shed light on the public and private life of the ancient Athenians. Noteworthy are some small bowls that contained hemlock, the official weights and measures of the city, the clepsydra for timing the speeches in the lawcourts, the jurors' metal tokens, the ballot-box used in the election of officials, and the decretal relief inscribed with the law against tyranny, of 336 BC. There is also a collection of black-figure and red-figure vases, as well as a significant number of *ostraka*. These last were potsherds on which the Athenians in the 5th century BC incised the name of whoever they considered a danger to the functioning of the democratic system. This took place during special assemblies of the Ekklesia of the Deme. The citizen whose name appeared on the largest number of *ostraka* was ostracized from Athens for ten years.

Other exhibits in the Museum of the Ancient Agora include coins (6th century BC-19th century AD), domestic vessels, terracotta lamps (7th century BC-11th century AD), as well as other works of the Hellenistic and Roman periods. Among the last a small collection of figurines, lamps, rattles and toys of Roman times is especially touching.

Ostraka (pot sherds) inscribed with the names of three leading personalities in the political life of Athens, in the first two decades after the Persian Wars: Aristeides, Kimon and Themistokles. All three were obliged to go into exile.

ANCIENT AGORA-ANCIENT AGORA MUSEUM

USEFUL INFORMATION

Opening hours
Tuesday-Sunday: 08.30-15.00
Closed Monday
Tel. of Ancient Agora Museum: 32 10 185

THE ROMAN AGORA

In the late 1st century BC donations from Julius Caesar and Emperor Augustus were used to build a new agora, commercial in character, to the east of the ancient Agora. Both marketplaces were linked by a wide paved street lined with porticoes. This street commenced at the Library of Pantainos and terminated at the impressive Gate of Athena Archegetes, on the west side of the Roman agora. During the Ottoman period this gate was a gathering place for vendors and peasants, who flocked to Athens from the villages of Attica for the annual fairs and the bazaars, hence its later name, Pazaroporta. A church of the Taxiarchs, built next to it in the 11th-12th century, was pulled down in 1843 and rebuilt a few years later. It is nowadays dedicated to the Panaghia (Virgin) Grigorousa. On the opposite, east, side of the Roman agora are traces of buildings dated to the 1st century AD. These are remains of Vespasians, that is public latrines, and possibly of the Agoranomeion, the headquarters of the market inspectors.

The horologion of Andronikos Kyrrhestes

The octagonal tower that stands on the east side of the

Julius Caesar, a man of remarkabe political and military abilities, played a decisive role in the history of Rome until his assassination on the Ides of March 44 BC. A Roman bust probably portraying Julius Caesar. Rome, Museo Nazionale

▶

art of the Roman Agora at Athens. This marketplace was rectangular in plan, comprising an internal court surrounded by porticoes with shops.

The 'Tower of the Winds', a monument that captured the imagination of European travellers in the 17th century, who called it 'Socrates' Tomb', while the contemporary Turkish traveller, Evliya çelebi, dubbed it 'Plato's Tent'.

▶ Depiction of the interior of the 'Tower of the Winds' during the Ottoman period. E. Dodwell, 1821.

The façade of Hadrian's Library, decorated with Corinthian columns. As Pausanias notes, the building had halls with gilded ceiling, statues and paintings.

teke, a Muslim house of prayer, for members of the sect of Mevlevid Dervishes.

THE **LIBRARY** OF **HADRIAN**

To the north of the Roman agora stands part of the magnificent library built by Emperor Hadrian in AD 132. The rectangular internal courtyard was surrounded by porticoes which fronted rooms specially arranged for storing bookrolls, for lectures and for

Roman agora was built in the second half of the 1st century BC by the astronomer Andronikos from Kyrrhos in Syria. A hydraulic clock, operated by water from the Acropolis, was installed in its interior, while marks of a sundial are preserved on the south side of the exterior. On the roof was a bronze weather-vane representing a triton, a mythical sea daemon with the body of a fish from the waist downwards. The frieze of the tower is decorated with reliefs of the eight winds, for which reason the Horologion of Andronikos Kyrrhestes is popularly known as the 'Tower of the Winds'. After the mid-18th century the ancient clock-tower became a

study. At the centre of the court was a cistern, which was later converted into an Early Christian basilica. This in its turn was replaced by the Megali Panaghia church, in the 11th century. During the Ottoman period the Upper Bazaar of Athens was located here. Its 100 or so shops were burnt down in a fire, in 1884.

ROMAN AGORA
USEFUL INFORMATION
Opening hours
Tuesday-Sunday: 08.30-15.00
Closed Monday
Address: 1 Aiolou St,
Plaka Telephone: 32 45 220

MONASTIRAKI

'The little shop in Athinas street (Monastiraki)'. Painting in acrylic by S. Vasileiou, 1970.

From Preclassical times till the reign of King Otto, the commercial hub of Athens was in more or less the same place. In the Ottoman period the market encompassed the sites of the Roman agora and Hadrian's Library as well as the streets around what is now Monastiraki Square. Areos street, then shaded by vines. Pandrosou and Iphaistou streets were full of haberdashery shops – selling ribbons, cloth and kerchiefs – and workshops of tanners, saddlers, blacksmiths and copper-smiths. Gradually, however, the focus of commercial life shifted to more recent streets in the city. Today booths selling antiques and folk art, as well as some quaint little coffee shops, have mainly remained in Monastiraki.

One of the picturesque streets in Monastiraki.

On the north side of Monastiraki Square stands the church of the Koimesis tis Theotokou (Dormition of the Mother of God) or the 'Pantanassa', which was from the late 17th century the heart of a monastery

The old Bazaar of Athens on the street that now passes in front of Hadrian's Library. Water-colour by E. Dodwell, 1805-6. Athens, Benaki Museum.

The mosque built by Voevod Jistaraki, at the busiest hub of the market of Ottoman-held Athens.

Painting of the Metropolis (Greek Orthodox cathedral) of Athens, which was consecrated in May 1862. Athens, Gennadius Library.

known as the Megalo Monastiri. For many years the monastery prospered, supplying the market with cloth woven by the monks. After the Greek War of Independence, however, it fell into decline and was eventually abandoned. Its name degenerated with its fortunes, from Megalo Monastiri, meaning great monastery, to the diminutive Monastiraki, i.e. small monastery. On the opposite side of the square is the Jistaraki Mosque, built in 1759 by the Ottoman voevod, the commander of the city. In order to construct it, Jistaraki's men demolished one of the columns of the temple of Olymian Zeus. This so angered the Pasha of Euripos, to whom Athens was subject adminstratively, that he order the voevod's banishment. In the same year there was a plague epidemic in the city and the Athenians blamed Jistaraki, for they believed that a misfortune is buried under every ancient column and is released when the column falls.

Very near the west side of Monastiraki is Avyssinias Square, venue of the traditional Sunday Flea Market, the Yusurum, which owes its name to a Jewish merchant, Noah Yusurum, who had a shop here. Since 1910, every Sunday morning Avyssinias Square fills with people looking for a bargain, from old gramophone records to antique furniture.

The Metropolis

The Metropolis or Greek Orthodox cathedral of Athens stands in Mitropoleos street, near the centre of the city. The foundation stone was laid in 1842 and the original plans were drawn by Hansen, the Danish architect to whom Athens owes many of its loveliest Neo-classical buildings. During the course of its construction, however, his designs were altered radically by the architects D. Zezos and F. Boulanger.

The Panaghia Gorgoepikoos

The small 12th-century church next to the Metropolis is dedicated to the Panaghia Gorgo-

epikoos (the Virgin the Fast-hearing). Its name has changed several times in the course of its history. When Queen Amalia, wife of King Otto, survived an assassination attempt, it was named Soteros (of the Saviour), while in 1862 it was 'baptized' Hagios Eleutherios. After the building of the Metropolis it was also called Mikri Metropolis (little cathedral). The lower section of its exterior is revetted with marble slabs, while incorporated in the masonry of the upper part is a host of ancient and Byzantine reliefs. It is a veritable sculpture exhibition. The Byzantine masons transformed the ancient reliefs into Christian ones by carving a cross between the pagan subjects.

Kapnikarea

Kapnikarea stands in Ermou street, one of the busiest shopping precincts in Athens. A charming Byzantine church dating from the mid-11th century, its name perhaps derives from its founders, the *kapnikarioi,* collectors of building tax in Byzantine times. In the 1940s the interior of the church was decorated with wall-paintings by the artists Kontoglou and Papanikolaou.

Hagioi Asomatoi

As the visitor continues down Ermou street, below Kapnikarea in the direction of the Kerameikos, he/she can admire the 11th-century Byzantine church of the Hagioi Asomatoi (Incorporeal Saints), in Asomaton Square.

THE KERAMEIKOS

'In the course of the same winter the Athenians, following the custom of their fathers, celebrated at the public expense the funeral rites of the first who had fallen in this war ... Any one who wishes, whether citizen or stranger, may take part in the funeral procession, and the women who are related to the deceased are present at the burial and make lamentation. The coffins are laid in the public sepulchre, which is situated in the most beautiful suburb of the city; ther they always bury those fallen in war ...'

(Thucydides, II xxxiv).

The cemetery in the most beautiful suburb of the city, as Thucydides describes it, was none other than that of the Kerameikos. This was the largest cemetery of Athens, extending *extra muros*, since burials were forbidden inside the city. Excavations have brought to light graves of different periods, a section of the city wall, sanctuaries, public and private

buildings and, of course, traces of the numerous potters' workshops that existed in the area and to which it owes its name (*Kerameikos* = Potters' Quarter). At one time two of the most important gates in the walls of Athens stood on the southeast side of the archaeological site. The first, the *Hiera Pyle* (Sacred Gate), was right beside the bed of the Eridanos, the rivulet that flowed through the Kerameikos in antiquity. The gate was thus named because it was the starting point of the *Hiera Hodos* (Sacred Way), the road taken by the procession of the Eleusinian Mysteries, which ended at the Sanctuary of Demeter at Eleusis. A short distance from the Sacred Gate was the *Dipylon Pyle* (Double Gate), the largest and most official entrance to Athens. Outside the Dipylon was the

One of the most impressive points in the archaeological site of the Kerameikos.

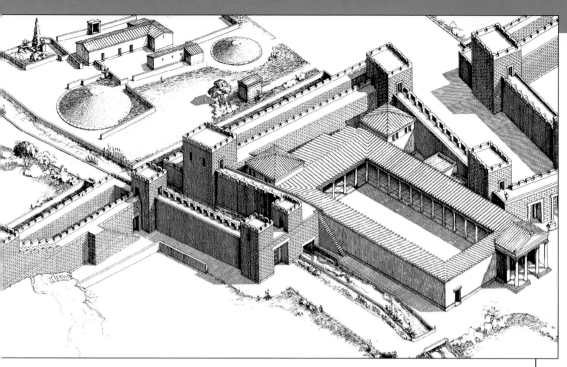

Reconstruction of the ipylon and the Hiera Pyle (Sacred Gate). Right the pylon in its earliest form, in the middle the earliest Pompeion, left the Sacred Gate and the river Eridanos, while visible beyond are the sanctuaries, pottery workshops and tombs.

The funerary stele of Hegeso, possibly a work by the famous sculptor Kallimachos. A replica of this stele now stands in the Kerameikos site, while the original is in the National Archaeological Museum, Athens.

Demosion Sema (Civic Cemetery), where citizens slain on the field of battle and those who distinguished themselves in Athenian affairs were buried at public expense. Most probably it was here that Pericles delivered his famous funeral oration, in honour of those killed in the first year of the Peloponnesian War. Discernible between the remains of the two gates are the foundations of the Pompeion, the building in which the sacred paraphernalia used at Athenian festivals were kept. It was here that every four years, on the 27th day of the month Hekatombaion, that is shortly before the middle of August, preparations were made for the procession of the Great Panathenaia. The following day, as dawn broke, the procession set off for the Acropolis. The

Pompeion in its earliest form was built in the late 5th century BC. It was destroyed by Sulla in 86 BC and rebuilt in the 2nd century AD.

To the southwest, near the church of Hagia Triada (Holy Trinity), the sanctuary of the Tritopatroi, that is the dead ancestors, was uncovered. Next to it are tombs of eminent Athenian families, adorned, in accordance with ancient custom, with funerary sculptures, vases and stelai. Although most of the splendid monuments we see are replicas of the original ones, they nevertheless evoke the tranquil atmosphere of the ancient cemetery. Among the most remarkable are the stele of Dexileos, final valediction to the young horseman who fell in battle near Corinth, in 394/93 BC; an imposing marble bull, eternal guardian of the family tomb of Dionysios of Kolyttes; the stele opposite, with the seated ethereal figure of Hegeso, who peruses a piece of jewellery while her maidservant stands before her (c. 410 BC).

THE KERAMEIKOS MUSEUM

The exhibits in this small but impressive museum come mainly from the site of the Kerameikos. Displayed in the first room are different types of Attic funerary monuments, from the Archaic period until the 4th century BC. Outstanding is the grave stele of Ampharete, protectively holding her dead grandchild in her arms, as well as the stele of Dexileos. Collected in other rooms are sepulchral vases and *ex-votos*, ranging in date from the 12th-11th century BC into Roman times. Of particular interest are the enormous Geometric amphorae, the white

▶

The funerary stele of the youth Dexileos from Thorikos in Attica. Dexileos is mounted on his horse, which rears up above the fallen foe at whom he directs his spear, now lost.

lekythoi, the miniature vases from children's graves and, in the last room of the museum, the hydria by the 'Meidios Painter', with its exquisitely depicted figures.

KERAMEIKOS-KERAMEIKOS MUSEUM
USEFUL INFORMATION
Opening hours
Tuesday-Sunday: 08.30-15.00
Closed Monday
Address: 148 Ermou St
Telephone: Kerameikos Museum: 34 63 552

The funerary stele of Ampharete, dated to 430/20 BC. The epigram incised on the upper part reads: 'Here I hold my daughter's beloved child, which I held on my knees when we alive saw the light of the sun and I the deceased now hold it dead'.

Area of the Olympieion

The Olympieion, located a short distance from the Acropolis, the sacred rock of the goddess Athena, is the sanctuary in which her father Zeus was worshipped. Ancient myths relate that Zeus, son of the Titans Rhea and Kronos, master of the world, once fought against his father and the other Titans. His allies in this struggle were his brothers Poseidon and Pluto, as well as other deities. The protracted conflict ended with the Titans' defeat. So Zeus won power and settled on Mount Olympos, from where he ruled over gods and men.

The Titan Kronos, son of Ge and Uranos, swallowed his children to prevent them taking power. Here the Titaness Rhea presents him with a swaddled stone instead of her late-born son, Zeus, which Kronos swallowed unawares. So Zeus was saved, and when he came of age he forced his father to regurgitate his brothers and sisters. Base, c. AD 160. Rome, Museo Capitolino.

THE OLYMPIEION

Sixteen columns are all that remain of the magnificent gigantic temple of Olympian Zeus, which once stood to the southeast of the Acropolis. This temple had a very checkered history. It seems that Zeus, first among the Olympian gods, was worshipped on this spot from early historical times at least. According to the archaeological evidence, an impressive temple dedicated to him stood here from the early 6th century BC. In the closing years of that century, around 517 BC, the grandson and namesake of the tyrant Peisistratos, Peisistratos the Younger, began replacing the old

▶ *Zeus, paramount god of heaven, was responsible for all changes in the weather, sending rain, hail, snow, thunder and lightning to earth. Here Zeus, proud and imposing, holds the sceptre in one hand and the thunderbolt in the other. Red-figure Panathenaic amphora, 480-470 BC. Berlin, Antikensammlung.*

temple with another larger and more luxurious one. Howevever, no sooner had he constructed the crepidoma, that is the base of the new temple, than the tyranny was dissolved. The Athenians, in their concerted effort to wipe out all reminders of the tyrants decided to discontinue the project. Several centuries later, in 174 BC, work on the Olympieion was resumed, at the expenses of Antioch IV Epiphanes, King of Syria. Thi time the temple was built to the height of the cornice, the section between the column capitals and the pediments. However, the king's death in 163 BC once again left it unfinished. It was finally completed by Emperor Hadrian, between AD 125 and 130. The splendid temple in the Corinthian order had 104 columns in all. Its dimensions, 110.35 m

long and 43.68 m wide, rank it among the largest temples in the ancient world. In its interior stood a colossal chryselephantine statue of Zeus as well as a portrait statue of Hadrian, whom the Athenians honoured as *symbomos* (sharing the altar) of Zeus.

Hadrian also built the sanctuary's large, rectangular *peribolos* (precinct wall), which is nowadays restored. Outside the *peribolos,* to the north, the ruins of houses (5th century BC-2nd century AD), a Roman balaneum (bath-house, 2nd century AD) and one of the earliest Christian monuments in Athens, a basilica of AD 450, have been excavated. Visible to ▶ the south of the sanctuary are remains of the temple of Apollo Delphinios (450 BC), protector of sea

voyages, adjacent to which were the lawcourts 'beside the Delphinion' (500 BC), where those who had killed in self-defence or by accident (manslaughter) were tried. Further east, remnants of a sanctuary dedicated to Kronos and Rhea have come to light (AD 150).

Emperor Hadrian's interest in Athens contributed to the reparation of the destructions caused by Sulla and the implementation of an ambitious building programme. Bust of Hadrian, 2nd century AD. Athens, National Archaeological Museum.

Hadrian's Arch, known in the Ottoman period as the 'Kamaroporta tis Vasilopoulas' (Doorway of the Princess's Chamber), had been incorporated in the wall built by Voevod Hadji Ali Haseki in 1778. At the time Athens was declared capital it was the official gateway to the town. It was here that Otto was welcomed in August 1834, a few months before he settled in Athens permanently.

View of Athens from the banks of the Ilissos. Watercolour by J.M. Wittmer, 1833. Athens, Benaki Museum.

HADRIAN'S ARCH

After the completion of the Olympieion the Athenians put up a triumphal arch in honour of Hadrian, to the northwest of the sanctuary. The emperor passed through this arch when he visited Athens in AD 131, to inaugurate the temple. Built of Pentelic marble, Hadrian's Arch is 18 m high. On its upper part are two inscriptions; the one visible from the side of the Acropolis reads: 'Here is Athens, the ancient city of Theseus', while the other, visible from the side of the Olympieion, where the city expanded in Roman times, reads: 'Here is the city of Hadrian and not of Theseus'.

SANCTUARIES ON THE BANKS OF THE ILISSOS

Once of a day the waters of the river Ilissos flowed to the south of the Olympieion. The bed of the river has been covered over by the roads of modern Athens. In antiquity important sanctuaries graced its banks, among them those of Aphrodite en Kepois (in the garden), Artemis Agrotera (the huntress) and the altar of the Ilissian Muses. The famous Kallirrhoe Fountain, the source from which Athenian maidens took water for their nuptial bath, was located in the same area. Further north, above the Panathenaic Stadium, there was a sanctuary of Herakles Pankrates, which means omnipotent. The name of the nearby

modern neighbourhood of Pangrati derives from this epithet. The verdant banks of the Ilissos were famed for their tranquility and idyllic beauty, extolled by Plato in his dialogue *Phaedrus*. He recounts that one summer day Socrates sat there under a shady plane tree with his pupil Phaidros and discussed the soul, love, philosophy and rhetoric.

The Zappeion building. Its garden was at one time the most popular place for a stroll in Athens.

THE ZAPPEION

The Zappeion is the Neoclassical building that stands on the opposite side of Vasilissis Olgas avenue, which skirts the north side of the Olympieion. One of the city's main exhibition centres, it was built under the auspices of the benefactor of the nation, E. Zappas. Building began in

Queen Amalia, wife of Otto and daughter of the Grand Duke of Oldenburg. Athens, National Historical Museum

1874, to plans drawn by the French architect F. Boulanger, but the Zappeion was given its present aspect in 1880, by the Dane Th. Hansen. It was he who designed its two principal features: the impressive propylon in the Corinthian order, the lovely column capitals of which are faithful copies of those on Lysikrates' Monument, and the internal circular court surrounded by a two-storey Ionic portico.

THE NATIONAL GARDEN

Behind the Zappeion spreads an enormous park, living memento of a bygone age. Work on laying out this garden commenced in 1840, at the behest of Queen Amalia, wife of King Otto, and the project was completed about a decade later. It was formerly

View of the National Garden.

Picture of the National Garden as it was laid out under the supervision of Queen Amalia, modelled on the garden in Munich. Athens, Gennadius Library.

known as the Royal Garden because at that time it belonged to the palace. Renamed the National Garden in 1923, this glorious park with its towering trees, small glades and ponds on which ducks nonchalantly swim, has been a favourite haunt of Athenians ever since. It is a perfect place for a leisurely stroll, especially on Sunday mornings in spring and summer.

SOTEIRAS LYKODEMOU

Opposite the west side of the National Garden, in Philellinon street, stands one of the most impressive Byzantine churches in Athens, dedicated to the Saviour, the Soteiras Lykodemou. Built in the 11th century, the church was badly damaged by an earthquake in

The church of the Soteiras (Saviour) Lykodemou or the Hagia Triada (Holy Trinity), as it was named after its restoration in the mid-19th century. The wall-paintings in its interior are by the Bavarian artist L. Thiersch.

1651, while parts of it were removed by the voevod Hadji Ali Haseki, in 1789, in order to build a defensive wall around the town of Athens, as it then was. Between 1850 and 1855, after the founding of the Modern Greek state, the church of the Soteiras Lykdemou was restored with donations from Tsars Nicholas I and Alexander II, and made over to the Russian community in Athens. For this reason it is often referred to as the Russian church.

THE PRESIDENTIAL PALACE

Situated in Irodou Attikou street, to the east of the National Garden, the palace was designed and built in the period 1891-1897 by E. Ziller, the gifted German architect who worked in Athens during the second half of the 19th century. It was originally the home of the Greek royal family, but after the restoration of democracy in 1974 it was designated as the official residence of the President of the Hellenic Republic. The entrance is guarded by evzones, soldiers in traditional costume with the *foustanela*, a kind of kilt.

THE PANATHENAIC STADIUM

The dazzling white marble stadium opposite the junction of Irodou Attikou street and Vasileos Konstantinou avenue, is built on the selfsame site as the ancient stadium of Athens, which

the traveller Pausanias (2nd century AD) described as: 'A marvel to the eyes, though not so impressive to hear of'. According to ancient inscriptions, the land here belonged to a private citizen, Deinias, who donated it to the city for the construction of a stadium. Around 330 BC Athens did indeed acquire its first stadium, work of the orator Lykourgos. Here the Athenians gathered to watch the games in which nude athletes participated, as part of the celebrations of the Great Panathenaia festival. In Roman times the stadium was revetted with white Pentelic marble, thanks to the generosity of Herodes Atticus, great benefactor of the city. Its capacity then was 50,000 spectators, while the dimensions of the track were 204.7 m long and 33.36 m wide. In the ensuing centuries the stadium fell into ruins. By 1869, when E. Ziller began excavating the site, all the marble had been used as building material in later constructions. Within a few years, however, it was restored to the splendour it had in the time of Herodes Atticus. It was revetted anew with

Representation of nude boy runners, from a 6th-century BC amphora. New York, Metropolitan Museum of Art.

Aerial photograph of the Panathenaic Stadium.

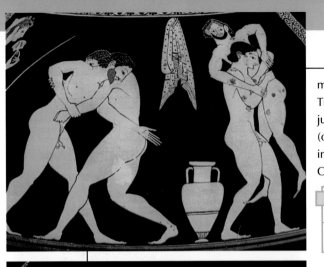

marble, at the expenses of G. Averoff. The Panathenaic Stadium, which is justifiably described as *kallimarmaron* (of beautiful marble), was inaugurated in 1896 to host the first modern Olympic Games.

Wrestling, the palaismosyne *of Homer, is one of the most ancient contests known. Above: two scenes of wrestling from a red-figure amphora of 530 BC. Berlin, Antikensammlung.*
Below: One wrestler, with a special hold, lifts up his opponent, trying to overcome him without touching the ground himself. Red-figure kylix, c. 430 BC. London, British Museum.

▶
The famous Discobolos by Myron, a work of around 450 BC, which was copied repeatedly during antiquity. Illustrated here is the best of these copies, the 'Lancelotti Discobolos', which dates from Roman times. Rome, Museo Nazionale Romano.

Representations of hoplitodromoi, that is runners who raced wearing helmet, greaves and holding a shield, from a 6th-century BC amphora. Munich, Staatliche Antikensammlungen und Glyptothek.

Area of the Parliament

On the night of 3 September 1834 a crowd of civilians and mutinous units of the regular army gathered in front of the royal palace, demanding that King Otto grant the nation a constitution. The king gave in to the pressure of events and agreed to their demand. This marked the end of the period of absolute monarchy in Greece. General Makryyannis, hero of the Greek War of Independence and one of the protagonists in the 3 September uprising, records in his memoirs that: 'I cared not for money and worldly goods, I wanted a constitution for my country, so that it will be governed by laws and not by personal whim'.

Painting inspired by the events of 3 September 1843. Colonel D. Kallergis, on horseback and head of the military, submits the rebels' demands to Otto and Amalia. Athens, L. Eftaxias Collection.

The impressive Neoclassical building that houses the Greek Parliament, originally the palace of King Otto and Queen Amalia, photographed at night. After the Greek catastrophe in Asia Minor, in 1922, Greek refugees from there were accommodated here.

THE GREEK PARLIAMENT

After the 1821 War of Independence Athens was merely a small town, desolated by conflicts between Greeks and Turks. Even so, in 1834 it was declared capital of the newly-founded Greek state. Rebuilding began at a rapid pace. One of the first new buildings was King Otto's palace, erected between 1836 and 1842 by the German architect Gaertner. Almost a century later, in 1831, the royal palace became the seat of the Greek Parliament.

In front of the Parliament is the monument to the Unknown Soldier, designed by the architect E. Lazaridis and the sculptors Ph. Rok and K.

Dimitriadis. It was unveiled on 25 March 1932. Guarded by evzones day and night, the monument bears a relief of a fallen ancient warrior, carved around which are the names of the places where the Greek army has fought in modern times, and excerpts from the 'Epitaph of Pericles'.

SYNTAGMA SQUARE

Opposite the Parliament lies one of the city's most famous squares. During the early years of Otto's reign it was known as Palace Square or the Garden of the Muses. After the events of 3 September 1843 it was renamed

The Parliament building and, in the small photograph, the Monument to the Unknown Soldier, with one of the euzones guarding it.

Syntagma (Constitution) Square. In 1842 a luxurious mansion was built on its north side, to plans by Th. Hansen. Originally the residence of the A. Dimitriou family, in 1874 it was turned into an hotel named the 'Grande Bretagne'. In 1960 the 'Grande Bretagne' was virtually demoliseed and rebuilt in the form it has today.

Constitution Square used to be surrounded by many traditional coffee shops, among them the legendary Zacharatos café, venue for impassioned political and literary discussions, and the Zavoritis cafe, owned by V.

Vasileiou. Vasileiou struck up a friendship with one of his customers, G. Zavoritis, driver of the steam-powered tram in Athens. Since both men were dissatisfied with their jobs they decided to swap them: Vasileiou became a tram-driver and Zavoritis ran a coffee shop, which he turned into one of the most popular in Athens.

▶ *Painting of Syntagma (Constitution) Square in the period of the interregnum (1862-1863). On the right is the A. Koromilas mansion, which was converted into an hotel after its owner's death. The Zavoritis coffee shop was in the ground floor of this hotel. Athens, Athenian Club Collection.*

The Neoclassical building designed by the architect A. Metaxas, which houses the treasures of the Benaki Museum.

THE BENAKI MUSEUM

The museum's founder, Antonis Benakis, was born in the Egyptian city of Alexandria in 1873. A cultured man of considerable fortune, he began his collection of ancient and later works of art while still in his youth.

When he settled in Athens in 1926 he decided to donate his invaluable collection to the state. Furthermore, he offered to house it in the wonderful Neoclassical mansion of 1900, which his father Emmanuel Benakis had purchased as the family home.

The museum, the life's work of Antonis Benakis, was inaugurated in 1931. Over the years the original collection has been enriched thanks mainly to the donations of private individuals.

Today's visitor to the Benaki Museum has the opportunity of admiring over 33,000 exhibits, a spectacular panorama of the Hellenic world, spanning its entire historical course. Of particular importance among the objects are the ancient, Byzantine and Postbyzantine

▶ Funerary portrait of a young man, from Antinoopolis in Egypt. Second quarter of 3rd century AD.

jewellery, the Byzantine relief icons, the Byzantine manuscripts, the wonderful Byzantine and Postbyzantine icons, the silver vessels and ecclesiastical treasures, as well as an assemblage of works from Egypt, including textiles, funerary portraits and exquisite bone carvings. Also displayed in the museum galleries are intricate embroideries from all regions of Greece, impressive woodcarvings, domestic objects, local costumes, paintings and sketches by foreign travellers, weapons and paintings of heroes and events in the 1821 War of Independence.

The Benaki Museum is involved in various cultural activities and operates a series of annexes or satellite museums. The most important of these are the building complex in the Kerameikos neighbourhood, at the junction of

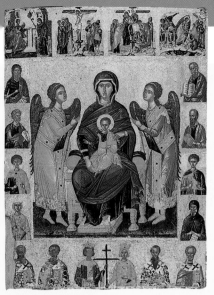

Icon of the enthroned Virgin and Child between two angels. Represented along the top are the Annunciation, the Crucifixion, the Descent from the Cross and the Resurrection. On the sides and bottom are saints, apostles and hierarchs. This splendid Cretan work of the second half of the 15th century is attributed to the famous painter Nikolaos Ritzos.

Vellum folio with depiction of the Three Boys in the Fiery Furnace, from Codex 49 of the Pantokrator Monastery on Mount Athos. The manuscript, which includes psalms and the New Testament, is dated 1084.

One of the museum's most important exhibits: panel of a triptych showing Christ blessing St John the Theologian. This small masterpiece of Cretan painting is dated around 1500.

Precious pendant in the form of a caravelle, from Patmos. One of the best-known and most-discussed pieces of jewellery in Greek lands.

The Adoration of the Magi, a work painted on a chest in the period 1560-1567, by the famous Cretan artist Domenikos Theotokopoulos (El Greco).

'The Greek Boy'. Oil-painting by A.M. Colin, 1829/30.

Wooden chest with painted decoration, from Mytilene. Late 18th-early 19th century.

The Flight into Egypt. A wonderful icon of Cretan art, second half of 15th century.

Dipylou and Asomaton streets, which houses the Islamic collections, and the Chatzikyriakos-Ghikas gallery at 3 Kriezotou street in Kolonaki. This is actually the former home of the great artist who introduced the European *avant garde* into Greek painting, and was bequeathed by him to the Benaki Museum. In addition to the personal effects and paintings by N. Chatzikyriakos-Ghikas, a collection of Chinese porcelain is exhibited there.

BENAKI MUSEUM

USEFUL INFORMATION

Address: 1 Koumbari St, Athens
Telephone: 36 11 617

Part of the interior of the reception room of an 18th-century mansion at Siatista. The exquisite workmanship of the woodcarved, gilded, silvered and painted decoration gives a vivid picture of the orientations of Greek art before the 1821 War of Independence.

View of the Stathatos Mansion, built by the architect E. Ziller and now the annexe of the Museum of Cycladic Art.

panels. Displayed in the cases on the ground floor are replicas of exhibits, which can be purchased from the museum shop.

First floor

This is devoted entirely to the remarkable culture that developed in the Cycladic islands after the Neolithic Age. The first period of the Bronze Age known as Early Cycladic in the islands, covers the period around 3200 till 2000 BC. The Cycladic islanders were engaged in seafaring and trade, and made elegant vases in clay or marble as well as tools and cosmetic objects. However, their most significan artistic creations are the marble anthropomorphic figurines, mainly female but also male. The development of these works is particularly interesting. The prehistoric sculptors progressed from the simple, abstract, violin-shaped figurines to more naturalistic representations and soon made the ground-breaking achievement of producing three-dimensional figures, such as the flute-player and seated harpist from Keros, in the National Archaeological Museum.

THE MUSEUM OF CYCLADIC ART

The Museum of Cycladic Art was established in 1986 by the N.P. Goulandris Foundation, whose aims are the study and promotion of Aegean Culture, in particular the culture of the prehistoric Cyclades. In addition to the ancient Cycladic works of art, the museum houses a large number of antiquities dating from 2000 BC to the 6th century AD, while its premises have expanded to the adjacent 19th-century Neoclassical building which was once the residence of Othon and Athena Stathatos.

▶

Front and back view of a marble female figurine, which is considered to be the most elegant of the Early Cycladic period. c. 2500/2400 BC.

Ground floor

Acquaintance with Cycladic Culture of the 3rd millennium BC begins from the museum foyer, through photographs, drawings and information

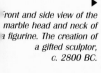

Stone-carving, an art that flourished in the Cyclades for a thousand years, declined sharply towards the end of the Early Cycladic period. The use and purpose of the figurines remains an enigma. Various theories have been expressed, such as that they were children's toys, amulets or cult effigies. Whatever their role, the Cycladic figurines are unique masterpieces of universal appeal. Two outstanding pieces in the Museum of Cycladic Art are the 'cup-bearer' and an impressive statue 140 cm high, distant ancestor of Archaic sculpture.

Second floor

Displayed here are works of art from different regions of Greece, dating from 2000 BC down to the 4th century AD.

Among the more interesting pieces are the clay vases and the gold and bronze jewellery ▶ from Skyros (Geometric period); the peculiar female plank-figurines from Boeotia (c. 590-500 BC); the bronze hydria with elaborate handle (450-440 BC); the 'eyed'

Front and side view of the marble head and neck of a figurine. The creation of a gifted sculptor, c. 2800 BC.

kylix on which wide-open eyes are painted, a motif probably attributed with magical properties to avert evil; the red-figure krater with the lively symposium scene (430 BC); the fish-plates decorated with fish and molluscs, from Southern Italy; the bronze vessels in excellent condition, donated to the museum by L. Eftaxias (8th century BC-1st century AD); a small shell-shaped vase (4th century BC); a small flask in the form of an acorn (400-390 BC); the marble statue of a laughing boy (320-310 BC) and, last but not least, two reliefs with representations of funerary banquets (*nekrodeipna*).

Third floor

A hall for lectures, seminars and temporary exhibitions.

Fourth floor

Exhibited here is the Karl Politis Collection, comprising 115 objects dating from the 14th century BC to the 6th century AD and including a series of impressive terracotta figurines. Outstanding among these are a very lovely Tanagraia figurines (late 4th-3rd century BC), an Ionian figurine of a maiden with elaborate coiffure and holding a fan (1st century BC), and a Late Hellenistic figurine of an actor with mask.

Marble goblet. The clear curving profile and the plasticity of the vase reveal a craftsman capable of bringing his material to life, c. 2700-2300 BC.

Stathatos Mansion

On the first floor are copies of plans and drawings by the architect E. Ziller, the Athens Academy Collection of ancient Greek art, reproductions of antique furniture and watercolours by J. Skene, inspired by Attic landscapes. There is also a multi-media installation with information on the exhibits in the museum. The second floor is used for temporary exhibitions usually of long duration.

MUSEUM OF CYCLADIC ART
USEFUL INFORMATION
Opening hours Monday-Friday: 10.00-16.00 Closed Sunday and Tuesday Address: 4 Neoph. Douka St, Kolonaki Telephone: 72 28 321-3

The 'Cup Bearer', c. 2700/2600 BC. The figure seated on a four-legged stool 'proposes a toast' with the cup in his outstretched right hand. Although the gender of the figure is not indicated, it is probably male, since all the extant examples of figures in action are male.

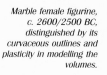

Marble female figurine, c. 2600/2500 BC, distinguished by its curvaceous outlines and plasticity in modelling the volumes.

Marble female statue 140 cm high and dated c. 2600/2500 BC. This work of monumental dimensions is a landmark in the history of sculpture worldwide.

Marble female figurine, c. 2600/2500 BC. The robust body, lyre-shaped head, angular sloping shoulders, carefully incised details and rounded back with no indication, as a rule, of the spinal column, are particular traits of figurines ascribed to the 'Goulandris Master', so named because the museum houses several of his numerous works.

arble female figurine, one of the masterpieces of Early Cycladic sculpture. The absence of knees is resumably due to the fact that it was broken in antiquity. Attributed to the 'Copenhagen Master' and dated c. 2600/2500 BC.

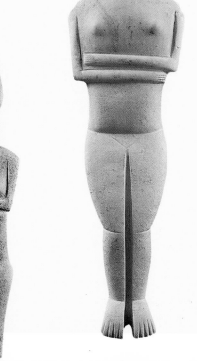

The villa of the Duchess of Plaisance to which the Byzantine Museum of Athens was moved in 1930. The villa was called the 'Ilissia' because the waters of the river Ilissos once flowed nearby.

THE BYZANTINE MUSEUM

A unique museum of its kind, which concentrates on the art that flourished throughout the vast Byzantine Empire from the founding of its capital, Constantinople, in AD 330, till its fall to the Ottoman Turks in 1453.

The history of Byzantine art, closely linked with events that determined the course of the empire, falls into four periods. The first, the Early Christian, commences in 330 and ends in the mid-7th century. This is followed by the Early Byzantine period, the time of the Iconomachy, the theological dispute between supporters (Iconodules) and opponents (Iconoclasts) of the depiction of

▶ *The Crucifixion. An outstanding example of icon-painting dated after the mid-14th century.*

Gravestone of the 4th-5th century AD, showing the mythical musician Orpheus in the midst of real and fantastic beasts which he enchants with his kithara (lyre). The representation must be of symbolic significance connected with immortality.

holy images and the veneration of icons, which lasted until the mid-9th century. The ascent of the Macedonian dynasty to the throne marks the end of this period and the beginning of the next, the Middle Byzantine. The Late Byzantine period began in 1204, the year in which Constantinople was sacked by the Crusaders, and ended in 1453. The break up of the Byzantine Empire did not mean the end of Byzantine art, however. The Byzantine artistic tradition lived on in the ensuing centuries, especially in those regions which were not subjected immediately to Ottoman rule. A striking example is Crete, which remained in Venetian hands until 1669. Between 1453 and 1700 the renowned Cretan School of painting enjoyed an ambit of influence that encompassed both East and West.

The Hospitality of Abraham. An icon representing a classical phase of Cretan painting in the first half of the 16th century.

The Virgin the Episkepsis. A 14th-century mosaic icon from Bithynia.

Crosier decorated with precious stones and enamel. It belonged to the Metropolitan of Adrianople, Neophytos (1653-1658).

Heptanesian icon of the 17th century, dedicated by Captain Ardavanis to the Virgin, who saved him from a shipwreck. The depiction of the Mother of God is combined with the scene of the wreck.

The Byzantine Museum was established in 1914. Housed originally in the Athens Academy, it was moved in 1930 to the complex of buildings erected between 1840 and 1848 by St. Kleanthis – or Th. Hansen according to a recent study –, for a French aristocrat, Sophie de Marbois, the Duchess of Plaisance. The museum's treasures, which will be re-exhibited shortly in newly constructed wings, include sculptures, icons, vestments, *objets d'art*, liturgical vessels and many more creations of Byzantine and Postbyzantine art. Noteworthy in the sculpture collection are the gravestone with representation of the mythical musician Orpheus, a closure panel with relief of the Tree of Life flanked by two lions (9th-10th century), a group of lion and antelope (9th-10th century BC) and a marble slab with figures of three apostles, from the Vlatadon Monastery in Thessaloniki (10th century). Other outstanding exhibits are the icon of Archangel Michael (14th century), the icon of the Crucifixion, from Thessaloniki (14th century), the important mosaic icon of the Virgin Glykophilousa (early 14th century), a series of double-sided icons dating from the 10th to the 15th century, the icon of the Hospitality of Abraham, an excellent example of the art that thrived in Crete after the Fall of Constantinople.

BYZANTINE MUSEUM
USEFUL INFORMATION
Opening hours
Tuesday-Sunday: 08.30-15.00
Closed Monday
Address: 22 Vas. Sophias Ave, Athens
Telephone: 72 11 027, 72 32 178

Gold-embroidered aer, that is a liturgical veil used initially to cover the Sacraments and later as an Epitaphios in Holy Week. An excellent work of art from Thessaloniki, it dates from the early 14th century.

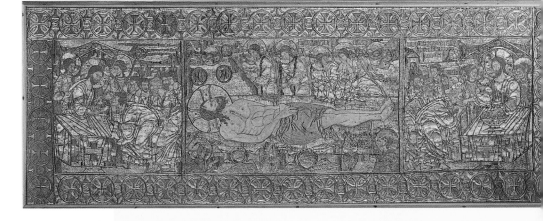

Early 13th-century wall-painting removed from a ruined church at Oropos. Depicted is a young deacon holding in his right hand a gold incense casket covered by a red encheirion.

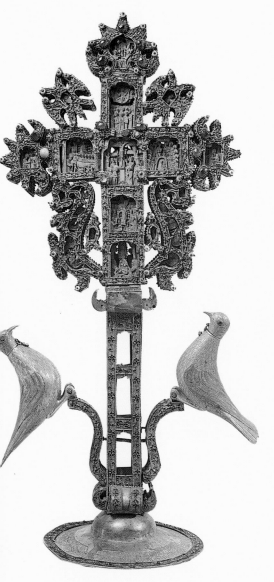

Large cross fashioned in 1654, decorated with enamel and woodcarved representations.

others house photographs and memorabilia from the Korean War and the Second World War, as well as field guns from the time of the First World War to the present. On the first floor are presentations of the martial aspect of each major period in Greek history. Of particular interest here are the prehistoric and Archaic weapons, the plaster casts of metopes from the frieze of the temple of Apollo Epikourios at Bassae in Phigaleia, the paintings with subjects inspired by the Greek War of Independence and the Second World War. The exit from the building leads to the outdoor exhibition areas, where there are cannon of different periods and military aircraft.

The War Museum was inaugurated on 18 July 1975. Its founding was prompted by the exhibition of the Martial History of the Greeks, presented in Athens between April and October 1968.

▶
Exhibited in the grounds of the War Museum are impressive military aircraft and a collection of cannon.

THE WAR MUSEUM

The Athens War Museum, housed in a heavy modern building next to the Byzantine Museum, is full of memories of military events, ancient and modern. Hung above the entrance are portraits of the freedom-fighters in the 1821 War of Independence. Displayed in the room to the right of the lobby is the Petros Saroglou Collection, which includes various types of weapons, dating from the 16th to the 20th century, mainly of Greek provenance but also from other parts of Europe and from Asia. The case at the far end of the room contains African bows and shields as well as cudgels and axes of primitive peoples. The basement hosts a collection of 19th- and 20th-century military uniforms. On the mezzanine floor, one room is dedicated to the Airforce while the

View of the National Art Gallery, building of which commenced in 1964 and was completed in 1975/76.

'The Crucifixion'. Oil-painting by El Greco. Mary Magdalene kneels and embraces the Cross, while the Virgin and St John the Evangelist stand right and left of the Crucified Christ.

▶

'The Concert of Angels'. Oil-painting by Domenikos Theotokopoulos. The representation of the heavenly orchestra crowned the scene of the Annunciation on a painting that was split into two pieces in the late 19th century. The main representation is in the Collection of the Urquijo Bank, Madrid.

THE NATIONAL GALLERY

The history of the National Gallery begins officially in 1900. However, the core of its collection started to be formed immediately after the Liberation of Greece, when Capodistrias was the first president of the newly-founded state. By the end of the 19th century a fair number of paintings had been amassed. Most of them were from donations, such as that of the lawyer and art collector Demetrios Soutzos, who bequeathed his entire fortune for the creation of an art museum. In the following years the National Gallery continued to enrich its collections and in 1954 it was

merged with the Alexander Soutzos Museum. A decade or so later, in 1976, the building in which it is housed today opened its doors to the public. The National Gallery's permanent collection includes sculptures, prints, minor objects, drawings, furniture, Western European paintings, a series of works by Domenikos Theotokopoulos (the famous El Greco, 1541-1614) and works by artists of the 18th-century Heptanesian School. However, the bulk of the exhibits are paintings by 19th-century Greek artists. Among the best known are Th. Vryzakis, whose source of inspiration was the War of Independence; Nikephoros Lytras, 'father' of Neohellenic painting; the landscape artist K. Volonakis; genre-painters N. Gyzis and G. Iakovidis. Greek 20th-century painting is represented by the *avant-garde* artists K. Parthenis and K. Maleas, the expressionist G. Bouzianis, N.

'Waiting'. Oil-painting by
Nikephoros Lytras. A
young girl, standing on
tiptoe, peeps out of the
window to see whether
her sweetheart is coming.
The charming scene is set
in the humble interior of a
Greek village house.

'Children's Concert'. Oil-
painting by Georgios
Iakovidis. Inside a German
house three child
'musicians' are trying to
amuse the baby held in its
mother's arms. The fourth
child, right, joins in the
concert by striking a glass.

Chatzikyriakos-Ghikas, N. Engonopoulos, S. Vasileiou, Y. Tsarouchis, Y.
Moralis, Y. Gaitis, D. Mytaras, A.
Fasianos and several others. In addition
to the permanent collection, the
National Gallery frequently hosts
temporary exhibitions, always of
outstanding interest.

'The Betrothal'. Oil-painting by
Nikolaos Gyzis. A many-figured
composition inspired by a common
event in Ottoman-held Greece.
Parents married off their sons and
daughters at an early age, in order
to save them from the compulsory
tribute of children.

'Theatre'. Oil-painting by Nikos Engonopoulos. Inside a room, two figures with masks flank a tailor's dummy with flowers in place of the head. A painting of peculiar character, on account of the contrasts created by its strong clear colours.

'Hillslope'. Oil-painting by Konstantinos Parthenis. An old man on foot and a young man on horseback, both dressed in tunics, advance towards a widening in a road. Behind them, the hillside projects through the foliage. This particular work marks a turning point in the development of the artist's style.

NATIONAL GALLERY
USEFUL INFORMATION
Opening hours
Monday, Wednesday-Friday 09.00-15.00, 17.00-21.00 Saturday: 09.00-16.00, Sunday: 10.00-15.00 Closed Tuesday
Address: 50 Vas. Konstantinou Ave, Athens
Telephone: 72 11 010, 72 35 937

'The Artist's Atelier'. Oil-painting by Nikos Chatzikyriakos-Ghikas. The artist remodels reality, through selective use of the achievements of Cubism.

'The Flood'. Fresco by Photis Kontoglou. Part of a mural decoration in the painter's house. At the centre is the Flood, on the left are the Five Gateways of Earth and on the right are ancient Greeks worshipping idols.

KOLONAKI

The 'aristocratic' quarter of modern Athens is famed for its boutiques with clothes by Greek and foreign designers, art galleries, bars, cafés and restaurants. In good weather the pavement cafés in Kolonaki Square are crowded, mainly with young Athenians sipping their coffee under the beaming Attic sun.

Moments of relaxation in Kolonaki Square. ▶

LYKAVITTOS

Lykavittos (Lycabettus), the highest hill in Athens, dominates the north side of Kolonaki. From antiquity till the 19th century it was arid and almost bare, with herbs and wild flowers the only vegetation. In 1890, however, on the initiative of the 'Woodlovers Association' (*Philodasiki Enosis*), it was planted with pine and cypress trees. Lykavittos can be ascended on foot, along the paths that wend their way up its densely wooded slopes, or by funicular railway, from the station at the top of Plutarchou street. On its summit is an old chapel of St George and the Lykavittos Theatre where plays and musical events

One of the fashionable pedestrian precincts in Kolonaki. ▶

The picturesque steps in Dexameni Square. ▶

Photograph of Athens. In the foreground, part of the Panathenaic Stadium, in the background, Lykavittos hill (275 m high), on the slopes of which was the source of the river Eridanos, tributary of the Kephissos.

On the summit of Lykavittos, the hill standing at the centre of Athens, is an old chapel dedicated to St George. The photograph shows it belltower, set against the background of the city bathed in sunlight.

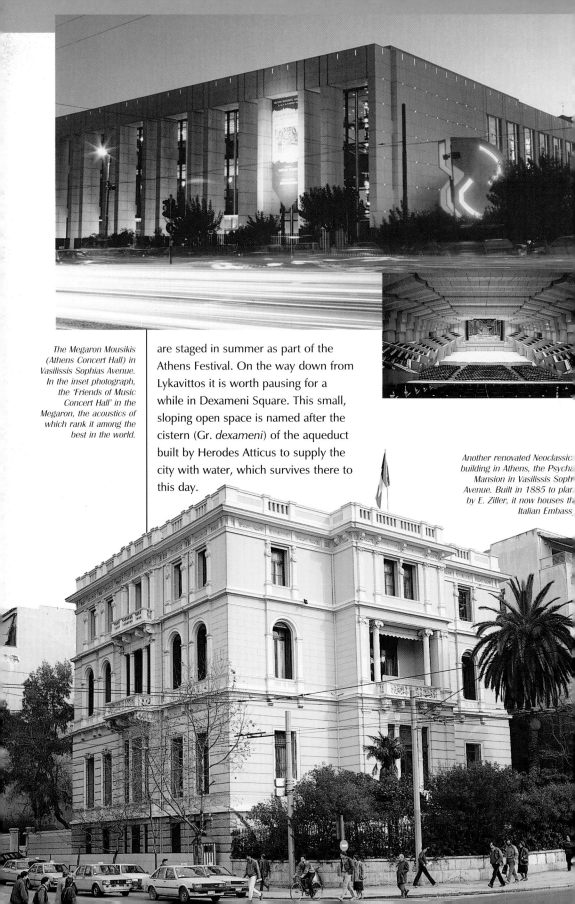

The Megaron Mousikis (Athens Concert Hall) in Vasilissis Sophias Avenue. In the inset photograph, the 'Friends of Music Concert Hall' in the Megaron, the acoustics of which rank it among the best in the world.

are staged in summer as part of the Athens Festival. On the way down from Lykavittos it is worth pausing for a while in Dexameni Square. This small, sloping open space is named after the cistern (Gr. *dexameni*) of the aqueduct built by Herodes Atticus to supply the city with water, which survives there to this day.

Another renovated Neoclassic building in Athens, the Psycha Mansion in Vasilissis Soph Avenue. Built in 1885 to plar by E. Ziller, it now houses th Italian Embass

By the mid-19th century, a few years after King Otto's arrival in Athens, the city and its inhabitants were already swept up in the pace of a new age. Athenians danced European dances for the first time, watched the first modern theatrical performances, took their first rides in horse-drawn carriages. Athens, with its countless ancient monuments, attracted architects from all over Europe. Wonderful buildings were erected everywhere, from the suburbs to the central thoroughfares, such as Panepistimiou (later E. Venizelou) avenue, where the country's first university was built, and Stadiou street, also known as 'acacia road' until 1911, when its fragrant acacia trees were felled in the name of progress.

THE UNIVERSITY

The three most characteristic Neoclassical edifices in the city — the Academy, the University and the National Library — were dubbed the 'Athens Trilogy' by Th. Hansen. The University was the first to be built, in 1839 to plans by Chr. Hansen, Th. Hansen's brother. Its painted decoration was begun in 1861 by the Bavarian artist K. Rahl and was continued after his death in 1888 by

The University, one of the oldest and loveliest public buildings in modern Athens.

the Pole E. Lebiedsky. A series of portrait statues was set up in front of the University: of the zealous patriot Rigas Ferraios, by the sculptor I. Kossos (1871); of Patriarch Gregory V, who was hanged by the Ottomans in Constantinople in 1821, by G. Phytalis (1872); of Adamantios Korais, mentor of the Greek Enlightenment, by G. Vroutos (1875); of the British philhellene and statesman W.E. Gladstone, by G. Vitalis 91885); of Ioannis Capodistrias, first president of Greece, by G. Bonanos (1928).

THE ACADEMY

Building of the Academy commenced in 1859, at the expenses of the benefactor of the nation, S. Sinas, and was completed in 1885. Designed by Th. Hansen, it is in the Ionic order with architectural details inspired by the Erechtheion. Statues of two gods,

Apollo and Athena, sculpted by L. Drosis, were set up on two tall Ionic pedestals in front of its façade.

THE NATIONAL LIBRARY

Building of the National Library, also designed by Th. Hansen but in the Doric order, began in 1887, at the expenses of P. Vallianos, and ended in 1902. The Library houses an enormous number of books, codices and incunabula.

ΠΡΟΣΟΨΙΣ ΠΡΟΣ ΤΗΝ ΛΕΩΦΟΡΟΝ ΠΑΝΕΠΙΣΤΗΜΙΟΥ
Ελίμαξ; 1ύω·λω·.

ΣΧΕΔΙΟΝ ΟΙΚΙΑΣ ΤΟΥ ΚΥΡΙΟΥ ΔΙΔΑΚΤΟΡΟΣ ΕΡΡΙΚΟΥ ΣΧΛΙΜΑΝΝΟΥ
ΑΡΧΙΤΕΚΤΩΝ Ε.ΖΙΛΛΕΡ.

Heinrich Schliemann's grand mansion, which now houses the Numismatic Museum, Athens. Athens, Cultural Centre of the Municipality of Athens.

THE 'ILIOU MELATHRON'/ NUMISMATIC MUSEUM

The loveliest of E. Ziller's creations in the Italian Renaissance style was built between 1879 and 1881 as the residence of Heinrich Schliemann, the amateur archaeologist who believed in the historical truth of the Homeric epics and discovered Troy, Mycenae and other major centres of the hitherto unknown Mycenaean civilization. Schliemann decorated the interior of his mansion with mythical opulence, while in every room, even the bathroom, texts from the ancient poets and authors were inscribed on the walls. The carved inscription 'Iliou Melathron', meaning palace of Troy, was placed on the building's façade.

The Old Parliament building, which now houses the National Historical Museum, with the equestrian statue of Th. Kolokotrinis in front.

In 1927 the Iliou Melathron became the property of the Greek state and for many years it was the seat of the Supreme Court. Today its carefully restored rooms, with their colourful murals, mosaic floors and painted ceilings, house the Numismatic Museum of Athens. Exhibited in this small, modern museum are coins of ancient, Roman, Byzantine and later times. The exhibits, the accompanying information panels and the multi-media installations are quite fascinating.

Silver stater (a silver coin valued at 2 drachmas) from Aegina, with representation of a turtle, c. 480 BC.

NUMISMATIC MUSEUM
USEFUL INFORMATION
Opening hours
Tuesday-Sunday: 08.00-14.20
Closed Monday
Address: 10-12 Panepistimiou St, Athens
Telephone: 36 43 774

The first railway line in the capital was opened in 1869 and linked Theseion with Piraeus. In this picture of Athens the steam-train has just left Theseion station and is heading for Piraeus.

NATIONAL HISTORICAL MUSEUM

The National Historical Museum is housed in the Old Parliament, one of the most important historic buildings in Athens. The original building belonged to the Chiote banker, A. Kontostavlos, but was purchased by the Greek state in 1836 and served as the palace of King Otto. In 1843 it began to be used as the seat of the Greek Parliament. A few years later, in October 1854, that building was burnt down. Rebuilding began in 1858, to plans drawn by F. Boulanger, and was completed in 1871, after modifications made to these by the architect P. Kalkos. Parliament continued to assemble here until 1931, when it was transferred to the Old Palace. The Old Parliament then housed the Ministry of Justice. In 1961 it became a museum. Exhibited in the galleries of the National Historical Museum are precious heirlooms from the time of the Fall of Constantinople (1453) to the modern age, presented in chronological order. These are mainly flags of various

▶

'Solon', woodcarved prow-figure in the form of the ancient legislator, from the early 19th-century sailing ship of the same name, owned by G. Panou from Spetses.

periods, such as those unfurled by Tz. Grigorakis in the Mani and G. Sisinis in Elis, in 1821; weapons, uniforms and portraits of heroes of the Greek War of Independence; helmets and suits of armour from the periods of Venetian rule and Ottoman rule; folk costumes; impressive jewellery from different parts of Greece; oil-paintings, watercolours, drawings and engravings with subjects inspired by recent Greek history. The museum also possesses personal effects of freedom-fighters, politicians, military officers, literati and prelates: individuals whose words and deeds left their indelible mark on the historical course of Hellenism. Among them are the weapons and helmet of Th. Kolokotronis, the lute of I. Makryyannis, the flintlock of A. Diakos, the desk of Patriarch Gregory V, memorabilia of Lord Byron and the desk of I. Capodistrias. Particularly intriguing is the collection of prow-figures, wonderful examples of folk woodcarving salvaged from ships that took part in the Struggle for the Liberation of Greece.

NATIONAL HISTORICAL MUSEUM
USEFUL INFORMATION
Opening hours
Tuesday-Sunday: 09.00-14.00
Closed Monday
Address: Stadiou & Kolokotroni St, Athens
Telephone: 32 26 370

Portraits of four heroes of the Greek War of Indepen-ence. Left, G. Karaiskakis, xt to him, Th. Kolokotronis the legendary 'Old Man of he Morea', and further on, he distinguished poet and hilhellene Lord Byron. Far right, one of the Greek women who took up arms against the enemy, Mando Mavrogenous, who was active in Mykonos.

KLAFTHMONOS SQUARE

The oldest of the central squares of Athens, about half way along Stadiou street, was known as Aischylou Square during the early years of Otto's reign. When the Mint was built here it was renamed Nomismatokopeiou (Mint) Square and after Otto was deposed in October 1862 it was called Eleftherias (Freedom) Square. Later, during the reign of King George I, the premises of the Mint were converted into the Ministry of Finance. At that time Greece was bedevilled by political instability and successive changes of government. With every change the civil servants were dismissed and replaced by others who were government sympathisers. The dismissed civil servants used to congregate outside the Ministry of Finance and weep, begging to be given back their posts. After one such gathering in 1878, the Athenian historiographer and writer D. Kambouroglou published an article in the magazine *Hestia*, in which he referred to the square as 'the garden of the weeper' (Gr. *klauthmonos*). It has been known by Athenians as Klafthmonos Square ever since, even though it was given the official name of Ethnikis Symphiliosis (National Reconciliation) Square in 1989.

HAGIOI THEODOROI

The 11th-century Byzantine church dedicated to the Sts Theodore stands at the northwest corner of Klafthmonos Square. Built on the site of an earlier church, it is interesting on account of the two donor inscriptions built into its front. The longer one records that the old dilapidated church was rebuilt by Nikolaos Kalomalos, while the shorter is inscribed with the date 1065.

Photograph of the Ambrosios Rallis residence in Klafthmonos Square. The mansion was built by the architect St. Kleanthis in 1837 and demolished in 1938. Athens, Benaki Museum.

Klafthmonos Square is also known as Ethnikis Symphiliosis (National Reconciliation) Square. This latter concept is symbolized by the huge statue by the sculpture Doropoulos, which dominates its centre.

One of the most important Byzantine monuments in Athens is the church of Hagioi Theodoroi, in Klafthmonos Square. It is of the cross-in-square type with dome.

The historic mansion of the Dekozis-Vouros family, which together with two adjacent mansions served as a palace for Otto and Amalia, for a few years. It now houses the very interesting exhibits of the Museum of the City of Athens.

▶

'Carnival in Athens'. Oil-painting by Nikolaos Gyzis.

THE MUSEUM OF THE CITY OF ATHENS

In 1833 the German architects G. Lüders and J. Hoffer built one of the first mansions in Athens, adjacent to the subsequent Klafthmonos Square. It belonged to the S. Dekozis-Vouros family and is also known as the 'First Palace' because it and two adjoining buildings served as the residence of Otto and Amalia from 1836 until 1843. The Dekozis-Vouros mansion was restored to its former glory in 1976, to house the Museum of the City of Athens/Vouros-Eftaxias Foundation, which is dedicated to the recent history of Athens. Its exhibits include several excellent paintings of Athenian

monuments and landscapes, antique furniture, vessels, an impressive maquette of Athens in 1842, made by the architect J. Travlos, King Otto's copy of the 1843 Constitution and a superb painting by N. Gyzis, entitled 'Carnival in Athens' (1892).

Area of Omonoia square

Once of a day, on the northern outskirts of the city, there was a tract of land full of vines and fig trees. In the first town plan of Athens it is noted as Othonos Square. After Otto was deposed, on 14 October 1862, the people of Athens gathered in this square, where they heard its new name for the first time, from the lips of the Prime Minister, D. Voulgaris: 'Let us swear upon this square, already given the lovely name *homonoia* (concord), and let each one of us say, I pledge loyalty to the fatherland and obedience to the national decisions ...'. Since that day Omonoia (Concord) Square has witnessed countless events that are part of Modern Greek history: rallies, street battles, political gatherings and celebrations of victories in sports.

OMONOIA SQUARE

View of the historic Omonoia (Concord) Square, the heart of the city for old Athenians.
▶

The aspect of Omonoia Square has changed many times since it was first laid out. Even so, some mementoes of the years of its heyday still fortunately survive. Two of them are the Alexander the Great (Megas Alexandros) Hotel and the Bangeion Hotel on its south side, both of which were built in the late 19th century by E. Ziller. Another building designed by Ziller stands at the entrance to the Square from Triti Septemvriou street. Since the time of the Balkan Wars its ground floor has housed one of the best-known old Athenian coffee shops, the 'Neon'.

The renovated building of the Town Hall (Demarcheion), one of the Neoclassical 'treasures' inherited by modern Athens.

DEMARCHEIOU SQUARE

The square opening off to the south of Omonoia Square was known in the early days as Loudovikou Square, in honour of the philhellene King of Bavaria, Ludwig, father of King Otto of Greece. Although its official name is Ethnikis Antistasis (National Resistance) Square, it is popularly called Kotzias Square or Demarcheiou (Town Hall) Square. The Town Hall of Athens, on the west side of Athinas street, was built between 1872 and 1874 by the architect P. Kalkos. The painted decoration of its interior was executed by the famous Greek artists Ph. Kontoglou and G. Gounaropoulos. Opposite, on the east side of Aiolou street, is the Dounados mansion, built in 1840 and converted between 1890 and 1895, and on the south side of the square is the Melas mansion, built in 1874 to plans by E. Ziller.

The centre of Demarcheiou Square was formerly dominated by the Civic Theatre of Athens. This famous theatre was founded in 1875 but because of financial problems took almost thirty years to complete. Its stage hosted many memorable performances by the most celebrated Greek and foreign actors. The Civic Theatre had a truly tragic end. It was demolished in 1939, on the

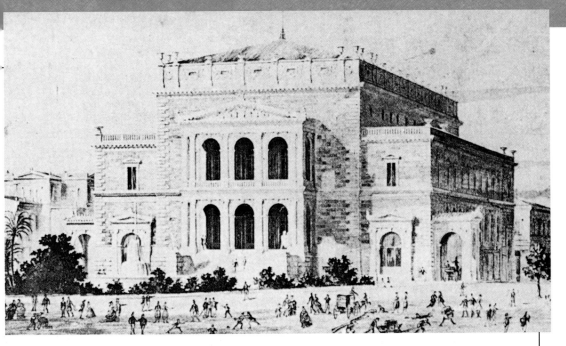

decision of the government minister and
prefect of Athens, K. Kotzias.

PSYRRI

*Miniature portrait of
Theresa Makri, from a
triple locket. Athens,
Benaki Museum.*

▶

One of the oldest 'working class'
neighbourhoods of Athens and
one of the eight 'terraces' into
which the town was divided
in the Ottoman period,
Psyrri is perhaps the only
quarter of the city in which a
picture of bygone Athens is
still very much alive. It is as if
time stood still here at the dawn
of the 20th century. Here, in Aghias
Theklas street, was the home of Teresa
Makri, the Athenian maiden with whom
Lord Byron fell in love and to whom he

*The foundation stone for the
famous Civic Theatre of Athens
was laid in 1857, to plans by F.
Boulanger, and the building
was completed in 1888, to
plans by E. Ziller. Photograph of
Ziller's plan for the Civic
Theatre. Athens, National
Historical Museum.*

*Two narrow streets in the
neighbourhood of Psyrri,
one the headquarters of
the disreputable* manges
and koutsavakides, *'wise
guys' and other members
of the Athenian
underworld. The 'state' set
up by the spivs of Psyrri
was broken
up by Police Chief
Bairaktaris in 1893.*

The National Theatre in Athens was designed by E. Ziller and modelled on the Dagmar Theatre in Copenhagen. The interior decoration was strongly influenced by that in the Volkstheater in Vienna.

wrote one of his best-loved poems 'Maid of Athens'. In recent years the long-neglected neighbourhood of Psyrri is being rehabilitated day by day, as its quaint little shops, grocery stores, leather workshops and carpentry workshops now coexist with *avant garde* theatres, post-modern bars and restaurants and *mezedopoleia* serving traditional Greek appetizers.

THE NATIONAL THEATRE

The foundation stone of the Royal Theatre of Athens was laid in Aghiou Konstantinou street in 1895 and the building was inaugurated with great pomp and circumstance in 1901. It was designed by the architect E. Ziller. At first it operated solely as an official royal theatre for a select invited audience. In 1908, however, it opened its doors to the general public. It was renamed the National Theatre in 1924.

THE POLYTECHNEION

The complex of Neoclassical buildings next to the National Archaeological Museum was designed and built between 1862 and 1876 by the architect L. Kaftantzoglou. The expenses were met by N. Stournaris, M. Tositsas and G. Averoff, who all hailed from the Epirote town of Metsovo, which is why the National Technical University of Athens is alternatively known as the National Metsovian Polytechneion.

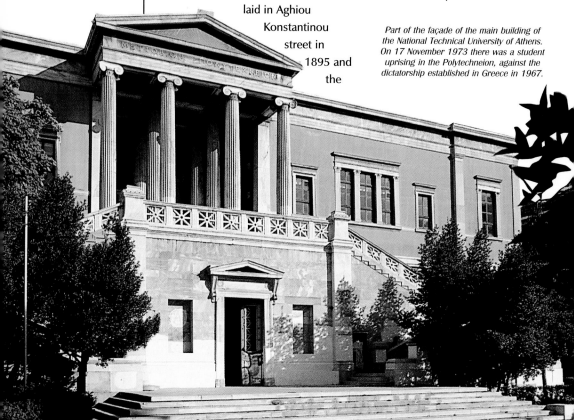

Part of the façade of the main building of the National Technical University of Athens. On 17 November 1973 there was a student uprising in the Polytechneion, against the dictatorship established in Greece in 1967.

Aerial photograph of the National Archaeological Museum.

THE NATIONAL ARCHAEOLOGICAL MUSEUM

From the dawn of prehistory the inhabitants of Greece felt the need to give concrete expression to their faith in the gods, their respect for the dead and their *joie de vivre*. Many of their creations were destroyed in the passage of time, but those which fortunately survived are now dispersed in museums and private collections in Greece and abroad. A very large part of these priceless objects is housed in the National Archaeological Museum, the most important museum of ancient Greek art in the country. Construction of the Neoclassical building which houses the National Archaeological Museum commenced in 1866, to plans drawn by E. Ziller, and was completed in 1889. On the oubreak of the Second World War the exhibits were packed in cases and stored in the basements of the building, buried under thick layers of sand. When the war ended the museum was renovated, enlarged and its treasures once again saw the light of day.

▶ The much-lauded gold death mask 'of Agamemnon', as it was called by Schliemann, who was the first to see it when it was recovered from Shaft Grave V at Mycenae, 1600-1500 BC.

Ground floor:
Prehistoric Collections.

These are exhibited in the first galleries of the museum. The largest, central gallery is full of Mycenaean artefacts, brilliant testimonies of the civilization that flourished on the Greek Mainland between 1600 and 1100 BC, and which was named after its main centre, Mycenae. The Mycenaean kings (Gr. *anaktes*) lived in imposing palatial complexes built on naturally fortified sites, from which they ruled their realm. When they died they were buried in the earlier phase in the shaft graves, while from the 15th century BC in monumental tholos tombs, the so-called 'treasuries'. Mycenaean art, known mainly from the graves and their contents, reveals influences from Minoan Crete. At the same time, however, it presents distinct peculiarities that echo the militaristic ethos of the Mycenaeans as well as their predilection for refined luxury.

The most important exhibits in the Mycenaean gallery were discovered in the royal shaft graves at Mycenae. These include exquisite inlaid daggers, such as that with a scene of men hunting lions and a second with a representation of running

Two gold cups with remarkable repoussé representations. Part of a treasure discovered in a tomb at Vapheio in Laconia, c. 1500 BC.

An impressive gold and silver rhyton – a ritual vase –, in the form of a bull's head. From Shaft Grave IV at Mycenae, 16th century BC.

▶

Elliptical bezel of a finger-ring from Tiryns, 1500-1400 BC. Represented are four leonine daemons, each holding a jug and advancing towards a goddess seated on a throne.

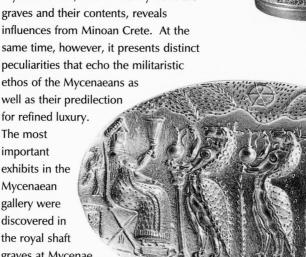

Marble Cycladic figurine a harpist, from Keros, a deserted island near Amorgos. This work of 2700 BC is considered to be one of the most splendid in Cycladic art.

Another exquisite work of art from Keros: a marble figurine of a flute-player, 2700 BC.

Lower part of a vase painted with a unique representation of fishermen. From Phylakopi on Melos, early 16th century BC.

lions; gold rings and seals with diverse devices; two elaborate vases (rhytons), one of gold in the shape of a lion head and the other silver in the shape of a bull head with gold horns; gold jewellery; gold funerary masks. Homer was fully justified in calling Mycenae *polychryses* (i.e. rich in gold). The same gallery also houses works from other major centres of Mycenaean civilization in the Peloponnese. Outstanding are the fragments of wall-paintings from the palace at Tiryns; two gold repoussé cups from Vapheio in Laconia; the clay Linear B tablets from the palace at Pylos. In the second gallery to the left of the central one, are vases, weapons, figurines, tools and jewellery dating from the Neolithic Age to the Early and Middle Bronze Age (3rd-2nd millennium BC), while in the small room next to it are finds from Kythera,

Ornate dagger decorated with three heavily-armed male figures and an enormous lion which has already pushed their companion to the ground. Further off, two other lions flee in fear. From Shaft Grave IV at Mycenae, 1600-1500 BC.

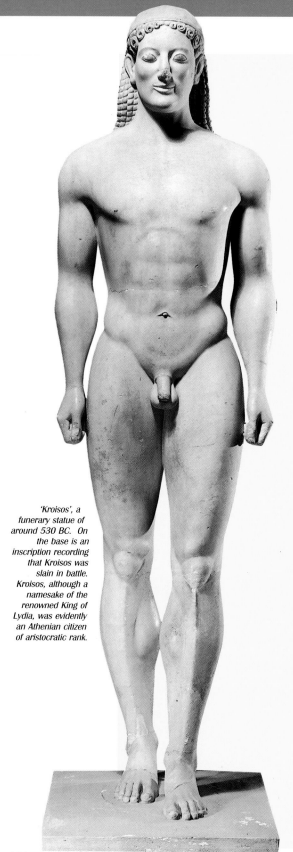

The relief of the 'hoplitodromos', c. 500 BC. A recent and widely accepted interpretation is that the youth is not in fact running in the hoplitodromos race but performing the pyrrhikios dance.

The votive relief of the 'Autostephonoumenos', c. 470 BC. It represents a young nude athlete placing the victor's wreath on his head. The wreath was apparently of metal, as the holes for affixing it to the marble indicate.

'Kroisos', a funerary statue of around 530 BC. On the base is an inscription recording that Kroisos was slain in battle. Kroisos, although a namesake of the renowned King of Lydia, was evidently an Athenian citizen of aristocratic rank.

Skopelos, Attica and other Mycenaean centres outside the Peloponnese. The third gallery, to the right of the central one, focuses on Cycladic culture. Outstanding exhibits here are the wall-paintings, vases and clay bathtub from Phylakopi on Melos, and two figurines, the flute-player and the harpist, from Keros.

Sculpture Collection.

This occupies a series of galleries, the first of which is to the left of the museum entrance hall. It is an

The 'Ilissos' grave stele, an excellent work of around 340 BC. A youth, half-seated on a grave stele, holds a lagobolos, a weapon used by hunters for catching hares. On the right stands his elderly father, his eyes filled with tears at his son's untimely death. The scene is completed by a hunting dog and the small slave boy who, exhausted by mourning, is curled up on the steps.

...rt of the bronze statue recovered ...m the sea bed in the bay of ...rathon, and hence known as the ...arathon Ephebe'. It may be a work ...the school of Praxiteles and is dated ...und 340-330 BC.

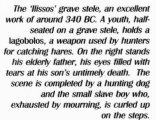

Detail of the 'Ilissos' stele.

enormous collection which presents the development of ancient Greek sculpture from the 8th century BC to the late 4th century AD. The most impressive of the Archaic creations are the *kouroi*, statues of nude young men which were set up as *ex-votos* in sanctuaries or as funerary monuments commemorating the dead; the statue of Artemis dedicated to the goddess by Nikandra from Naxos; the statue of Phrasikleia; the grave stele of Aristion; the stele of the *hoplitodromos* (runner in a race for armed foot-soldiers - hoplites). The Classical period is represented by wonderful works, landmarks in the history of art, such as the Melos disc; the relief of the *autostephanoumenos* (man crowning himself with a wreath); the bronze statue of Poseidon found in the sea off Cape Artemision; the colossal relief of Demeter, Persephone and Triptolemos; the Diadoumenos by Polykleitos; the bronze horse and jockey, again from the sea off Cape Artemision, the ephebe (youth) from Marathon; the

ephebe from Antikythera and the numerous fragments of sepulchral monuments. We cite indicatively the stele of Mnesagora and her little brother Nikochares; the lekythos from Myrrhina; the stele of Hegeso; the stele of Polyxenes; the Ilissos stele; the *naiskos* of Aristonautes. Noteworthy among the Hellenistic sculptures are the bronze head of a philosopher, recovered from the sea bed off Antikythera; the statuette of a naked boy holding a duck; the statue of Poseidon from Melos; the sculpted group of Aphrodite, Pan and Eros. The collection concludes with works from the Roman period, including busts of Emperor Hadrian, and of his favourite, Antinoos; of Herodes Atticus and of his beloved pupil Polydeukes; and a wonderful portrait of a youth with idealized features.

Bronze Collection.

Gods, warriors, athletes, *korai*, *kouroi*, *Nikai*, animals and a host of other figures compose the museum's collection of bronzes. The majority of the pieces were votive offerings of

Marble state of c. 100 BC, a copy of the famous 'Diadoumenos' sculpted by Polykleitos around 430 BC. It has been argued that the work represents a hero or an athlete who is tying the victor's ribbon round his head after winning some contest.

Bronze statue of c. 180 BC, recovered from the sea off Cape Artemision in Euboea. The horse, galloping swiftly, is ridden by a boy-jockey of inderterminate nationality. He is perhaps a negro, like many slaves and grooms in ancient Greece.

Magnificent temple-shaped sepulchral monument of c. 310 BC. The dead, who according to the inscription on the archtrave was called Aristonautes son of Archenautos from Halaia, is represented in panoply with his chlamys fluttering behind him, poised to attack the enemy.

Small painted pinax of around 540 BC, with representation of a procession leading a lamb to the altar for sacrifice. It was discovered in the Pitsa Cave, Corinthia.

Attic Geometric amphora, c. 755-750 BC. The main subject of the decoration is the prothesis *(lying in state) of the dead.*

pilgrims to the major sanctuaries and date from the 8th to the 4th century BC. The K. Karapanos Collection, with finds from the Necromanteion at Dodone (8th c. BC -3rd c. AD) holds pride of place.

Egyptian Collection.

This includes statues, figurines, sarcophagi, mummies, vases and many other artefacts, dating from the 5th millennium to the 1st century BC.

Stathatos Collection.

The most precious section of the collection of ancient and Byzantine works of art donated to the museum by Helen Stathatos is the Hellenistic gold jewellery.

The rest of the halls on the ground floor are used for lectures and temporary exhibitions.

First floor:
Vase Collection.

This spans a long period, from the 11th to the 4th century BC, the most productive for ancient Greek vase-making and vase-painting. Some of the memorable works in the collection date from the Protogeometric (1050/1025-900 BC) and the Geometric (900-700 BC) periods, as well as the phase of the "Orientalizing" style (700-630 BC), thus named because of the wide use of decorative motifs of Eastern provenance. Unique achievements are the Attic black figure and red-figure vases, decorated with subjects inspired from the world of myth and of everyday life, and the white lekythoi, vases for funerary use. Last but not least, particularly interesting are the Corinthian and Boeotian vases, the terracotta decoration from the Archaic temple at Thermos in Aetolia and the small polychrome plaques from the Pitsa cave in the Corinthia.

Attic white lekythos, c. 10-400 BC. The dead is depicted in front of his tomb.

Thera Gallery.

The central gallery of the first floor is devoted to the prehistoric site at Akrotiri on Thera (Santorini), a cosmpolitan centre of international trade that enjoyed its heyday in the first half of the 2nd millennium BC and was destroyed around 1650 BC by a tremendous eruption of the island's volcano. In the front section of the room are examples of the pottery, bronze vessels and tools, and stone objects characteristic of the flourishing culture at Akrotiri, and a plaster cast of a wooden bed. Placed at the far end of the room are some of the splendid wall-paintings that adorned the luxurious two- and three-storey houses of the Bronze Age city.

red-figure epinetron, a special vessel used by women for carding wool. This is the most richly corated example known. Attributed to the Eretria Painter, 425-320 BC.

Atrium:

Exhibited here are sculptures from different periods, such as a huge

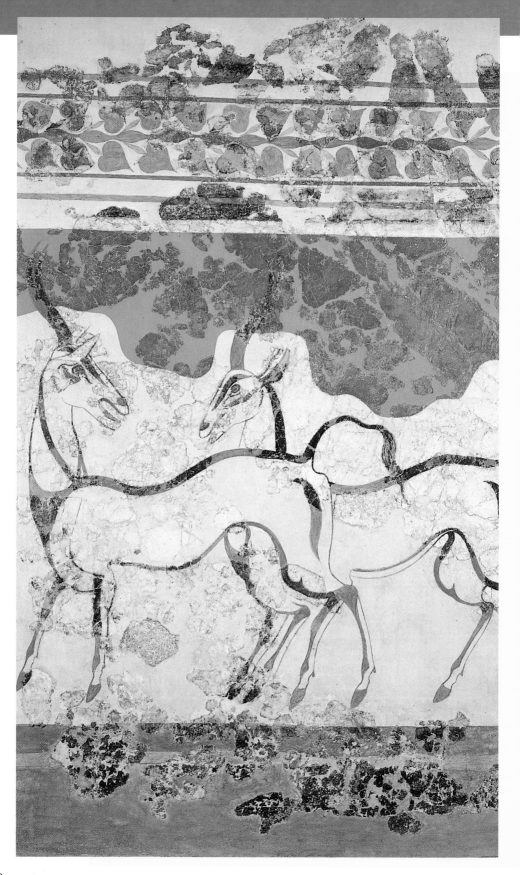

...elopes, part of a wall-painting of c. 1650 BC ...n Akrotiri, Thera. ...e of the masterpieces ...Theran art. Using the ...ic colours black ...d white, the talented ...nter has rendered ...e exotic animals with ...uralism and precision, ...ch perhaps indicates ...t he had travelled ...oreign parts and ...erved them at first ...d.

Boxing Boys, part of a wall-painting from Akrotiri, Thera, c. 1650 BC. The lively moment reveals an interesting aspect of social life in the prehistoric Cycladic settlement.

The 'Lilies' or 'Spring Fresco', from Akrotiri, Thera. The artist depicted a rocky landscape at the time of year when lilies bloom and swallows mate. Dated c. 1650 BC.

sarcophagus of the 3rd century AD and statues recovered from the Antikythera shipwreck.

THE EPIGRAPHIC MUSEUM

The largest museum of its kind in the world with some 13,500 inscriptions dating from the 8th century BC into Early Christian times. The overwhelming majority are Greek but there are some written in Latin and in Hebrew. Not all the galleries are open to the general public. Even so the visitor cannot fail to admire the enormous range of inscriptions, from fiscal lists of the Athenian League to honorary decrees and accounts kept by overseers of building works on the Parthenon and the Erechtheion.

▶
Detail of the 'Lilies' or 'Spring Fresco'.

In the Athens area

PIRAEUS

In the 6th century BC, when Athens had not yet developed into a major naval power, its port was at Phaleron. Myth relates that it was from there that Theseus set sail for Crete and Menestheus for Troy. It was Themistocles who realized the advantages of the location and terrain of the Piraeus and persuaded the Athenians to transfer their outport here. So the common historical course of the two cities began. Construction of the defensive wall round the new port in 493 BC, the year that Themistocles was elected archon, and was completed in 479 BC, after the end of the Persian Wars. Themistocles' fortifications were added to later with the building of the Long Walls that linked Athens with the Piraeus. In the mid-5th century BC the Piraeus was enlarged on the basis of plans prepared by the renowned town-planner and architect Hippodamos from Miletos. The Athenians' defeat in the Peloponnesian War naturally affected the fortunes of their port. The most important consequence was the demolition of its walls, which were rebuilt a few years later, by Konon in 393 BC. The next major catastrophe for the Piraeus was its destruction by fire in 86 BC, by the Roman general Sulla. This coincided with the start of its decline. In the Middle Ages and the Ottoman period Piraeus was no more than a humble village. At that time it was known as Porto de Leone, after the large marble lion, memento of its past glory, which stood beside its central harbour. A replica now stands there in its stead, because the original was taken to Venice by Morosini in 1688. Piraeus remained a backwater until Athens was declared capital of Modern Greece in 1834. Since then it has developed rapidly and is now not only the largest port in Greece but also among the major ports of the Mediterranean. The principal

Depiction of the harbour of Piraeus as it was in 1837, that is the time of its revival. Visible left is the customs house (Dogana). Athens, National Historical Museum.

feature of Piraeus was and is its three natural, sheltered harbours: Kantharos – the central one, Zea – today's Pashalimani, and Mounichia – now known as Mikrolimano or Turkolimano. In ancient times Kantharos was a commercial harbour *par excellence*. On its east side, today's Akti Miaouli, there were five large commercial stoas. One of these was called Deigma because there the merchants displayed samples (Gr. *deigmata*) of their wares. On the opposite side of the harbour are remains of the Eetioneias, one of the monumental gates in the wall of the Piraeus, close to which a

splendid sanctuary dedicated to Aphrodite Euploias, protectress of seafaring, was founded. In contrast to the Kantharos harbour, Zea was the basic naval station for Athens. On its northwest side part of the foundations of one of the most important buildings in the Piraeus has been revealed. This was the Skeuotheke, built around 330 BC by the Eleusinian architect Philon to house the equipment for the warships, such as sails, oars, anchors and ropes. The third harbour of the Piraeus, Mounichia, was also for military purposes. Excavations in the area have brought to light the sanctuary of Artemis Mounichia, next to the present Yacht Club building. The great Piraean festival in honour of the goddess, the Mounichia, included a procession and boat races. At the summit of the acropolis of Mounichia, the present neighbourhood of Kastela,

Dominating the central harbour is the station of the electric railway line, one of the most noteworthy examples of Neoclassical architecture in Piraeus.

Kastela hill, a particularly fascinating neighbourhood overlooking the waters of the Saronic Gulf.

The impressive building of the Piraeus Civic Theatre, designed by D. Lazarinos and modelled on the Opéra Comique in Paris, was inaugurated in April 1895.

was the sanctuary of a Thracian goddess, Bendis, who was akin to Artemis and had been included in the Athenians' pantheon. Only scant traces of the rest of the ancient buildings in the Piraeus have survived, among them remains of the shipsheds (*neosoikoi*), that is shelters in which the ships were kept, and parts of the fortification wall erected by Konon. There are ruins of a theatre of the 2nd century BC, to the west of Zea, at the height of Philellinon street, as well as of a second, larger and earlier theatre, on the north slope of Kastela. There is another ancient monument to the northwest of the Peiraiki Akti, beside the sea. This is a grave enclosure next to which stands a columns some 9

metres high. It is believed to be the burial place of Themistocles, from where he could 'watch' the ships and the rowing races organized in his day in the Piraeus.

Piraeus in the 21st century is a busy city. Thousands of passengers pass through its central harbour daily, on ferry boats and cruise ships, while in the neighbouring marinas hundreds of speedboats and sailing yachts are moored. The streets of Piraeus are lined with shops, restaurants, bars and cafés. In many places restored Neoclassical mansions stand majestically beside the modern high-rise blocks. Surely the most magnificent of all the old buildings is the Civic or Municipal Theatre, built in the late 19th century, in Vasileos Georgiou street. Piraeus has a special character and atmosphere, which can be discovered by wandering around its suburbs, strolling though the Sunday bazaar in the area of Ippodameia Square and of course visiting Kastela hill with its superb view, and picturesque Mikrolimano with its waterfront tavernas serving fresh fish.

Squadron of Byzantine warships sailing in fair wind. Picture painted and donated by N. Kalogeropoulos. Piraeus, Maritime Museum of Greece.

▶

THE PIRAEUS ARCHAEOLOGICAL MUSEUM

The museum houses archaeological finds from the port of Piraeus as well as from other sites in Attica and the islands of the Saronic Gulf. Its galleries are filled with sculptures. Some of the most impressive are an eagle which probably stood on a soothsayer's tomb (late 4th c. BC), a series of relief plaques of the mid-2nd century AD and the unique temple-shaped sepulchral monument of Nikeratos son of Polyxenos (c. 330 BC). Outstanding among the exhibits on the first floor are the finds from the Minoan sanctuary on Kythera (c. 1500 BC), some objects of everyday use, such as toys, mirrors and medical instruments, the vase collection and the remarkable bronze statues of Athena, Artemis and Apollo. Last, of interest is the gallery that has been modelled in the form of the front of a typical ancient temple.

The 'Piraeus Apollo', a bronze statue of around 510 BC that was discovered in Piraeus, along with other unique works of art such as the statue of Artemis, in 1959. The god is represented in the type of the Archaic kouros, except that his right leg is to the fore and not the left. Piraeus, Archaeological Museum.

THE MARITIME MUSEUM OF GREECE

Its two thousand or so exhibits bring to life the maritime history of Greece from prehistoric times to the present day. The majority of pieces are models of ships both ancient, such as the triereme *Olympias*, and modern, such as the battleship *Psara* which took part in the Balkan Wars (1912-1913). There are also numerous memorabilia, maps, weapons, flags and pictures, including an impressive oil-painting by K. Volanakis depicting the Greeks setting fire to a Turkish ship in 1821. An additional attraction in Gallery C is part of the Themistocleian Wall, which has been incorporated in the fabric of the museum building.

Excellent bronze statue of Artemis, the goddess of hunting, perhaps a work by the sculptor Euphranor, c. 350 BC. Piraeus, Archaeological Museum.

PIRAEUS ARCHAEOLOGICAL MUSEUM
USEFUL INFORMATION
Opening hours
Tuesday-Sunday: 08.30-15.00
Closed Monday
Address: 31 Charil. Trikoupi St, Piraeus
Telephone: 45 21 598

MARITIME MUSEUM OF GREECE
USEFUL INFORMATION
Opening hours
Tuesday-Saturday: 09.00-14.00
Closed: Sunday-Monday
Address: Akti Themistokleous-Phreattydos Square, Piraeus
Telephone: 45 16 264

The façade of the katholikon of the Monastery of Kaisariani or Syriani. The first testimonia relating to the monastery give both names. The Metropolitan of Athens, Michael Choniates, in a letter dated 1209, calls it Kaisariani, whereas Pope Innocent III, in 1208, refers to it as Santa Syriani.

KAISARIANI MONASTERY

On the west slope of Mount Ymittos (anc. Hymettos), tucked away in a vale verdant with pine, plane and cypress trees, is one of the most important Byzantine monuments in Attica, the Kaisariani Monastery. Although the area has not been investigated systematically, signs of human occupation in the Neolithic Age have been noted. However, most of the archaeological finds from Kaisariani date from the Classical and Roman periods. Some of these, such as columns, column capitals and reliefs, are scattered in the monastery courtyard, while others have been used as construction material in the katholikon and other buildings. There is interesting information on the area in the ancient authors, from whom we learn that in their day the slopes of Mount Hymettos were renowned for their philosophical schools, delicious honey and three springs. Indeed, the ancient Greeks believed that the water from the 'Kyllos Peras' spring cured sterility. Several historians have identifed the 'Kyllos Peras' with the Kalopoulas spring, to the northeast of the monastery, since its waters were attributed with the same properties in later times. The early history of the monastery is still obscure. However, it was apparently flourishing in the late 12th-early 13th century. At that time, as well as later, until the 18th century, it was a significant spiritual and intellectual centre, with a very rich library. It was also a prosperous foundation, deriving much of its income from honey production. When Athens was captured by the Latins in 1204 the Abbot (hegumen) of Kaisariani swore allegiance to the Pope and the monastery thus remained free and was exempted from taxes. Something similar must have happened later, at the beginning of the Ottoman Occupation. Tradition has it that when Mohamed the Conqueror visited Athens in 1458, the abbot presented him with the keys to the city. In return, the sultan waived all the monastery's fiscal obligations. It merely had to pay the Ottoman governor of Athens a token sum annually. By the late 18th century the monastery had declined.

A little later, in the early years of Otto's reign, Kaisariani and its entire property passed into the possession of the Greek state.

Today's visitor to Kaisariani first beholds the high wall surrounding the monastery, giving it a fortress-like aspect. On the east side of the internal courtyard, as one enters the complex, stands the katholikon, a characteristic late 11th-century Byzantine church dedicated to the Presentation of the Virgin in the Temple (Eisodia tes Theotokou). Its walls are of cloisonné masonry, i.e. built of stones of equal size, each boxed in by red bricks. Its narthex, i.e. west section, was added in the 17th century, the side-chapel (parekklesion) of St Anthony in the 16th and the bell-tower in the 19th. Of particular interest in the interior of the church are the four ancient columns upholding the dome, as well as the early 18th-century wall-paintings. The wall-paintings in the narthex are slightly earlier and were executed in 1682 by the Peloponnesian painter Ioannis Hypatos 'at the expenses' of the Athenian nobleman Benizelos, who had taken retreat with his family in Kaisariani, to avoid some pestilence in the city. This is narrated in the dedicatory inscription preserved on the west wall, above the entrance to the narthex. Ranged around the internal courtyard are the other buildings of the monastery: the refectory, the kitchen, the monks' cells and the bath-house (*loutronas*), an 11th-century building

The katholikon of the Kaisariani Monastery is of complex inscribed cruciform type or, according to another view, a semi-complex four-columned church. The photograph shows the outside of the dome, which is distinguished by its sparse decoration.

which continues the architectural tradition of the Roman thermae. During the Ottoman period this installation was converted into an oil-press.

The Kaisariani Monastery suffered much damage and was pillaged many times over the centuries. When the War of Independence was declared in 1821 the contents of its famous library were taken to the Acropolis, then under siege by the Turks, and used as ignition paper for the Greek blunderbusses. The monks' cells have long been deserted, but the monastery still has that calm, spiritual atmosphere which is only felt in a holy place.

KAISARIANI MONASTERY

USEFUL INFORMATION

Opening hours
Winter: Tuesday-Sunday 08.300-15.00
Summer: Tuesday-Sunday 08.00-14.30
Closed Monday
Telephone: 72 36 619

DAPHNI MONASTERY

Maidens with candles accompany the Virgin and her parents, Joachim and Anna, to the temple. Detail from the Presentation of the Virgin in the Temple, depicted in the narthex of the katholikon of the Daphni Monastery.

In ancient times a temple dedicated to Apollo Daphnaios or Daphnephoros stood about half way along the Sacred Way (*Hiera Hodos*) that linked Athens with Eleusis. In the 5th century AD a Christian church was built on exactly

General view of the Daphni Monastery, which is one of the most interesting examples of Byzantine architecture surviving in Attica.

the same spot. This church was the nucleus of Daphni, the oldest and most important monastery in Attica. The name Daphni may well derive from the epithet of Apollo, but other versions of its etymology link it with the Daphni Monastery at

Constantinople, or with a queen called Daphne, who in popular lore is said to have founded the monastery after surviving a shipwreck off Skaramanga. In the reign of Emperor Justinian I (527-565) Daphni enjoyed a great heyday. There followed a long period of desertion, lasting until the 7th or the 9th century. Its fortunes changed in the 11th century, when the monastery experienced a second floruit. The ruined katholikon was rebuilt and its interior decorated with polychrome marbles and wonderful mosaics. In 1207, after the conquest of Athens by the Latins, Otto della Roche ceded Daphni to the Catholic Cistercian Order. Orthodox monks did not return there until several centuries later, during the Ottoman Occupation. The monastery was subsequently evacuated several times, to escape raids by Turks or pirates, but was never totally abandoned. Later, during the 1821 War of Independence, the Greek freedom-fighters took refuge here. Daphni was also used as an ammunition store by the Turks, a barracks by Bavarian soldiers and even as a lunatic asylum. Its adventures came to an end in 1888, when excavations and restoration works commenced. The visitor to the

Christ, left, and St John the Theologian, right. Details from the scenes of the Entry into Jerusalem and the Crucifixion, respectively, which adorn the north cross arm of the church.

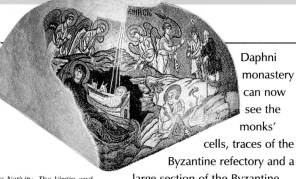

The Nativity. The Virgin and the baby Jesus are depicted in the mouth of the cave, with Joseph right, two shepherds above and four angels on the roof of the cave. One of the four representations framing the image of Christ Pantocrator.

Christ Pantocrator, whose imposing, expressive figure dominates the dome of the church.

The south side of the katholikon of the Daphni Monastery. Visible is part of the small paved court which was laid some time in the Ottoman period, after 1458.

Daphni monastery can now see the monks' cells, traces of the Byzantine refectory and a large section of the Byzantine fortification wall. It goes without saying that the most magnificent building in the complex is the katholikon, dedicated to the Dormition of the Virgin (Koimeses tes Theotokou). An 11th-century church of octagon type, its principal feature is the enormous dome that covers virtually the entire interior. For all its size, the dome appears remarkably light, due to the 16 windows opened in its drum. In the early 12th century an exonarthex was added to the narthex. At one time the exonarthex had a second storey, which housed the abbot's apartments or the library. Without doubt the uniqueness of the katholikon at Daphni is due to its splendid mosaic decoration. Depicted high on the walls of the nave (naos), the esonarthex and the sanctuary are archangels, saints, prophets, martyrs and hierarchs, as well as scenes from the Life of Christ and the Life of the Virgin. The dome is dominated by Christ Pantocrator, surrounded by 16 prophets in the lunettes. Of the original representations in the church 76 have survived to this day, some intact and some damaged. Even in this depleted state the spectacle they present is quite overwhelming. The harmonious

colours, the graceful well-proportioned figures, the modelled drapery of the garments and the diffuse nobility of the countenances, all reveal why the Daphni mosaics are considered the finest creations of the Middle Byzantine period.

DAPHNI MONASTERY

USEFUL INFORMATION

Address: end of Hiera Hodos
Telephone: 58 11 558

ELEUSIS

From most ancient times Demeter, goddess of fertility and protectress of cereals, was worshipped at Eleusis (mod. Elefsina) together with her beloved daughter Persephone. According to myth, one day Persephone was picking flowers with her friends in a meadow, when suddenly the earth opened and from its depths Pluto, god of the Underworld, emerged on his chariot. He seized the girl and brought her to his kingdom, to make her his wife. When Demeter heard her daughter's mournful cries, she set off to roam the earth, disguised as an old crone. She wandered for nine days and nine nights, until she came to Eleusis, where she was received in the palace of King Keleos. After revealing her true identity, the goddess asked the Eleusinians to build a temple for her. She then shut herself inside it, lamenting the loss of her beautiful daughter, and not a single seed sprouted on Earth. When Zeus heard what had happened, he decided to intervene and both parties therefore agreed that Persephone would spend one third of the year with her husband and the remaining months with her mother, who in her joy let the earth bear fruit. The Eleusinian Mysteries, the most important of the rites celebrated in honour of Demeter, were associated initially with the fertility of the earth and later with the pursuit of happiness in this life and the life after death. All those initiated in the cult swore absolute secrecy concerning what they had seen, heard and been taught. The punishment was harsh for those who broke this vow. When, one night in 415 BC, the drunken Alcibiades disclosed the secret acts to non-initiates, he was condemned by default to death. So, even though the Mysteries attracted devotees for almost 1500 years, very little is known about them.

The Lesser Mysteries, the first stage of initiation, were celebrated in Spring, in

View of the sanctuary of Eleusis, one of the most important religious centres of antiquity. Here the faithful gathered to be initiated into the Eleusinian Mysteries, the rites of which have been kept a closely guarded secret over the centuries.

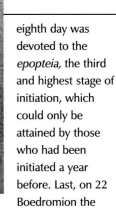

the month of Anthesterion (March), in the sanctuary of Demeter and Kore en Agrais (in the fields), close to the river Ilissos. The Great Mysteries followed, in the month of Boedromion (September) and lasted nine days, that is the duration of Demeter's wanderings. On the first day, 14 Boedromion, sacrifices were made at Eleusis. Then a large procession was formed, headed by the priestess of Demeter, with the *hierophantes,* the chief priest of the Mysteries, behind her. The procession followed the Sacred Way and terminated at the Eleusinion en Astei (in the city), at the foot of the Acropolis. Over the next four days there were sacrifices and other rituals, such as the purification of the faithful in the sea at Phaleron. On the sixth day the procession departed on its return journey to Eleusis. The Eleusinians awaited the devotees on the bridge over the Sarandopotamos, and bantered them with taunts, the so-called 'gephyrismoi' (*gephyra* = bridge). The faithful had to restrain themselves from retorting in anger, suffering the ordeal in silence and thus demonstrating their faith. On the night of 20 Boedromion, the second stage of initiation commenced, inside the Telesterion at Eleusis. Nothing is known about the content of the rites, except that some re-enacment took place, perhaps of the Abduction of Persephone (the *dromena*), secret phrases were uttered (the *legomena*) and the sacred objects were revealed (the *deiknymena*). The

eighth day was devoted to the *epopteia,* the third and highest stage of initiation, which could only be attained by those who had been initiated a year before. Last, on 22 Boedromion the initiates made libations to the dead and on the 23 each one left for home, with the fear of death allayed and expectations of a better life.

The earliest finds from the excavations in the area come from a Middle Bronze Age (1900-1600 BC) settlement and cemetery. The worship of Demeter seems to have begun in the next period, the Mycenaean, since a small Mycenaean building was uncovered in the northeast corner of the Telesterion. Presumably the first temple of the goddess, this was incorporated in the later one. At the beginning there was a local cult, but it became panhellenic over time and later, under Roman rule, drew devotees from all over the then known world. In Solon's day (early 6th c. BC) the Mysteries were included, by

According to mythology, Triptolemos, King of Eleusis, made the first plough– with the help of Demeter and Persephone – and learnt to till the earth, to sow seed, to reap corn and to thresh it. He then set off to travel the world, teaching men how to cultivate grain. In this representation the two goddesses, Demeter (left) and Persephone (right), initiate the young Triptolemos into the Eleusinian Mysteries. Votive relief, 440-450 BC. Athens Archaeological Museum.

A running kore, figure from the pediment of the temple at Eleusis. The statue's findspot and the diadem on its head suggest that Persephone herself is represented or one of the maidens who was with her when she was abducted by Pluto. c. 490 BC. Eleusis, Archaeological Museum.

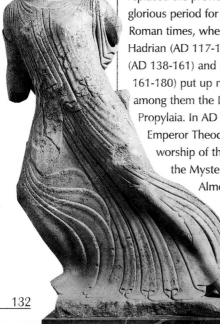

special law, in the festivals of Athens. A Telesterion, known as the Soloneion, was built then, as well as a large sacred precinct (*peribolos*). In Peisistratos' day (550-510 BC) the Solonian Telesterion was replaced by another more spacious edifice, while a strong defensive wall was also raised, transforming Eleusis into a fortress of Athens. During the Persian Wars, in 480 BC, the sanctuary was razed to the ground by the enemy army. The rebuilding of the Telesterion, which remained unfinished, and the enlargement of the sanctuary after the Persian Wars are projects attributed to Kimon. In the second half of the 5th century BC Eleusis was apparently included in Pericles' ambitious building programme. The sanctuary was extended even further and a splendid new Telesterion, designed by Iktinos, replaced the previous one. The last glorious period for the sanctuary was in Roman times, when the emperors Hadrian (AD 117-138), Antoninus Pius (AD 138-161) and Marcus Aurelius (AD 161-180) put up numerous buildings, among them the Lesser and the Great Propylaia. In AD 379, an edict of Emperor Theodosius banned the worship of the ancient gods and the Mysteries began to decline. Almost two decades later, in AD 395, a Goth invasion, led by Alarich, reduced the Eleusinion to rubble. The echo

of the hymns of the devotees still reverberates in the sanctuary of Demeter, but there are only scant remnants of its buildings. In front of the entrance to the archaeological site lies a Roman court, paved with rectangular marble slabs. In about the middle of this court there once stood a temple dedicated to Artemis Propylaia and Poseidon Patroos, while to the right and left of it were two triumphal arches of Roman times. Beside the arches were baths, thermae and inns, and next to the east arch was a fountain of the first half of the 2nd century AD. Visible beyond are the remnants of the Great Propylaia, an exact copy of the central section of the Propylaia on the Athenian Acropolis. At its northeast corner is the so-called 'Kallichoron phrear', the 'Well of the Good Dances', believed in Classical times to be the place where Demeter had sat to rest when her peregrinations brought her to Eleusis. In the first half of the 1st century AD the Lesser Propylaia, the entrance to the sanctuary proper, was built next to the Great Propylaia. A short distance away, next to a cave in the rock, a triangular *peribolos* was uncovered, and the foundations of a small building of the 4th century BC, which has been identified as the temple of Pluto. Tradition has it that the gateway to the Underworld, Hades, opened here. Further south stood the Telesterion, the most sacred and significant building at Eleusis, which could accommodate 3000 people. In the period 317-307 BC a stoa built by the Eleusinian architect Philon was added to its east side. The remaining area of the sanctuary was occupied by several other buildings, such as temples, stoas, a bouleuterion of the 4th century BC, a Roman gymnasium and a cistern, as well as storerooms for the grain that was offered by the faithful to Demeter and Persephone every year.

Votive relief of the 4th century BC. Left, Artemis, sitting on a rock, receives the pilgrims coming to revere her, 'arktoi' included among them. Brauron, Archaeological Museum.

THE ELEUSIS MUSEUM

The museum was built in 1889 to house finds from the excavations in the sanctuary and in the west cemetery of Eleusis. Exhibited in its six rooms are sculptures, vases and works in the minor arts of various periods. The most impressive of these are the amphora with the scene of the Blinding of Polyphemos; the 'Fleeing Kore'; a headless statue of Demeter of *c.* 420 BC, ascribed to the sculptor Agorakritos; the colossal statue of Kore with a *cistus* (sacred casket) on her head, from the Lesser Propylaia; the clay and stone *kernoi* (ritual vessels) in which offerings to the goddesses — wheat, lentils, honey, wine, oil — were placed. In the fourth room there are two plaster maquettes, one of the sanctuary as it was in the 6th century BC, and another with its aspect in Roman times. Last, sculptures are exhibited in the museum courtyard, among them a marble sarcophagus of the 2nd century AD.

Triptolemos, sitting in a winged chariot, gazes at Persephone who holds a flaming torch and a jug for libations. Behind him stands Demeter, with a torch and ears of wheat in her hands. Red-figure skyphos, 480 BC. London, British Museum.

ELEUSIS–SANCTUARY AND MUSEUM
USEFUL INFORMATION
Opening hours
Winter: Tuesday-Sunday 08.30-15.00
Summer: Tuesday-Sunday 08.00-14.30
Closed Monday
Address: 1 Gioka St, Eleusina
Telephone: 55 46 019

BRAURON

The area of Brauron (mod. Vravrona), on the east coast of Attica, was first inhabited in the Late Neolithic period, c. 3500 BC. The prehistoric settlement flourished during the Middle Helladic and the early phase of the Mycenaean period. Later, after the Geometric period, it began to decline gradually. In contrast, the local sanctuary, whose history began in the late 8th century BC, enjoyed ever increasing influence. The sanctuary of Brauron was dedicated to Artemis, protectress of nature, wild animals, childbirth and new-born babes. It was also closely associated with Iphigenia, daughter of Agamemnon, who was going to be sacrificed to Artemis so that the ships of the Greeks could set sail for Troy. At the final moment, the goddess snatched her from the altar and led her to the land of Taurus. On returning to Greece, Iphigenia and her brother Orestes brought the cult of Artemis to Brauron. According to a local myth, Iphigenia remained in the sanctuary for the rest of her life. It was to her that the garments of women who had died in childbirth were offered. Those women who had delivered safely dedicated their garments to Artemis, as a token of gratitude.

At Brauron, as in other ancient sanctuaries, festivals were organized in honour of the goddess. The most important of these was the Brauronia, celebrated every four years. Among its various events were contests between bards (rhapsodists) who recited epic poems. The impressive procession that

set off from the sanctuary of Artemis on the Acropolis and ended at Brauron was also part of the Brauronia. The best preserved building in the archaeological site of Brauron is a Π-shaped porticoed building, the so-called Stoa of the Arktoi, the young girls and boys,

Votive relief of the 4th century BC. Left, Artemis, sitting on a rock, receives the pilgrims coming to revere her, 'arktoi' included among them. Brauron, Archaeological Museum.

mainly of Athenian families, whose parents had promised them to the goddess before their birth. The Arktoi, from 5 to 10 years of age, lived in the sanctuary for a certain period of time and took part in the cult rites. Representations on vases of the 6th and 5th centuries BC show that they danced around the altar, clad in saffron-coloured chitons and holding flaming torches. The name Arktos derives from the Greek word for bear, the sacred animal of Artemis.

To the west of the Stoa of the Arktoi is a stone bridge of Classical times and further south is part of the foundation of the temple built *c.* 485

▶

Statue of a delightful little 'arktos' holding a dove, 4th century BC. Brauron, Archaeological Museum.

BC. Remains of buildings brought to light on a rock overlooking the temple of Artemis have been identified as the sanctuary and tomb of Iphigenia. Worship of Artemis at Brauron ceased in the 3rd century BC, when her sanctuary, one of the most revered in Greece, was badly destroyed by floods and abandoned. A few centuries later, the pagan religion was supplanted by Christianity. During the Early Christian period, 6th century AD, a basilica was erected to the west of the sanctuary, and several hundred years on, in the 16th century, the small chapel dedicated to St George was built.

THE BRAURON MUSEUM

The museum houses mainly impressive finds from the sanctuary of Artemis at Brauron, such as vases, jewellery, sealstones, sculptures. However, objects from Porto Rafti, Merenda, Anavyssos and other parts of the Mesogeia are also displayed. The most outstanding exhibits are the votive reliefs from Brauron, of the the 5th and 4th centuries BC, and the statues of the Arktoi.

BRAURON-BRAURON ARCHAEOLOGICAL MUSEUM

USEFUL INFORMATION

Address: Vravrona, Markopoulo, Attica
Telephone: 0292/ 39363

135

SOUNION

When the world was shared out after the battle between gods and Titans, Poseidon, son of Kronos and Rhea and brother of Zeus, was declared lord of the seas. Poseidon, like all the great gods, had a splendid palace on the summit of the sacred mountain, Olympos. But his real kingdom lay in the depths of the sea, where a second palace, built of gold, awaited him. There he spend his days and nights in the company of his wife Amphitrite. He frequently journeyed over the waves on his golden chariot, while dolphins sported merrily around him. The worship of Poseidon was widespread throughout the Hellenic world. The Athenians, desirous of honouring the god who had laid claim to the patronage of their city, dedicated to him a magnificent sanctuary at the southeast tip of Attica, on Cape Sounion. The Sounion peninsula, inhabited since prehistoric times, seems to have been established as a religious centre in the 8th century BC or possibly earlier. Homer is the first to mention Sounion as 'sacred cape of Athenians' and recounts that here Menelaos buried Phrontis, the worthy captain of his ship, on returning from the Trojan War. In the early 5th century BC construction of a majestic poros temple on the highest point of the promontory began. Work was never completed however, because in 480 BC the invading Persians reduced it to ruins. As the ancient historian Herodotus informs us, after the naval battle of Salamis the Athenians set up on Sounion one of the Phoenician ships that they had captured, so that all would remember their glorious victory. Later, shortly after the mid-5th century BC, the temple still partially preserved today was built on the site of the earlier one. Constructed entirely of pristine white Agrileza marble, the later temple, in the Doric order, had 6 columns on the narrow sides and 13 on the long, as well as a frieze decorated with representations of the Gigantomachy, the Centauromachy and the Labours of Theseus. The name of the architect who designed the temple is not known, but it is suspected that he was also the creator of three other famous temples: of Hephaist s in the Agora at Athens, of Ares at Acharnai and of Nemesis at Rhamnous. There was a *peribolos* around the temple of Poseidon, with a monumental propylon on its north side. Two stoas were built along the north and west sides of the sacred precinct, in which pilgrims could

Sunset over Sounion. The majestic ruins of the ancient temple overlooking the Aegean have inspired many artists, such as Byron, who sung Sounion's praises in three of his poems.

Terracotta Corinthian pinax painted with a warship carrying hoplites. An ex-voto found in the sanctuary of Athena Sounias, 7th century BC. Athens, National Archaeological Museum.

shelter from the blazing sun or the torrential rain. In antiquity Sounion was not only of religious importance but also of tremendous strategic significance. The Athenians accordingly transformed it into one of the principal forts of Attica. The entire sanctuary was

surrounded by an enceinte, reinforced with square towers, which prevented access from the north and west.

Recent studies have shown that the original wall was built in 412 BC, at a critical phase for the Athenians in the

Peloponnesian War, and that considerable additions were made in the 3rd century BC. Excavations inside the fortress, though sporadic, have shown that it was filled with the houses of soldiers and priests, as well as of citizens of the ancient deme of Sounion. To the west, at the point where the wall is closest to the sea, remnants of shipsheds (neosoikoi) are visible. Warships were kept on the alert here, to be launched in emergency situations. Northeast of the fortress, some 500 metres away, a second sanctuary has come to light. Here Athena was worshipped as protectress of Athens. Investigations at this site have revealed traces of two temples. The first, a singular marble building in the Ionic order, with colonnades on just two sides, the south and the east, was built in the Classical period and transferred to the Athenian Agora during the reign of Emperor Augustus. The second, which is smaller, was formerly considered to be earlier, dating from the Archaic period. However, it is

The colonnades and cella of the magnificent temple dedicated to Poseidon by the Athenians. It is only natural that as the naval power of their city grew, so did the importance of worshipping the god who ruled the seas.

▶

Part of the colonnade of the temple of Poseidon. The first investigations were made here in the late 18th century, while the first systematic excavation was conducted by the German W. Dörpfeld in 1884. Later excavations and studies of the site by the Greek Archaeological Society led to the conclusion that the temple was dedicated to Poseidon and to the discovery of the neighbouring sanctuary of Athena.

nowadays believed that it was contemporary with the first or slightly later, and that it was dedicated to the goddess Artemis, patron deity of miners. The silver mines of Laurion, one of the most important sources of wealth for ancient Athens, are only a short distance from Sounion. So it is very possible that the temple was erected by a lessee of mines. A smaller and earlier temple discovered adjacent to that of Athena perhaps belonged to the hero Phrontis. After the end of the Classical period Sounion gradually declined. In the troubled years of Byzantium, particularly the 14th century AD, it was used as a pirates' lair. The ancient temple was by then in ruins but some of its columns were still standing. So sailors who espied it from afar called the headland Cavo Kolones. In more recent times this isolated corner of Attica was visited by

travellers, anonymous and famous, among them Lord Byron who carved his name among the countless graffiti on one of the antae of the entrance to

the temple. All of them came here with one desire, which is shared by today's visitors, to see at close hand the legendary 'marble height' and the enchanting view over the open sea to the Aegean islands.

Colossal statue of a young man, known as the 'Sounion Kouros', c. 600 BC. It was discovered together with parts of other Archaic kouroi, buried in a repository (apothetes) near the temple. These kouroi, ex-votos of wealthy mariners and merchants, were set up in the sanctuary prior to its destruction by the Persians in 480 BC. Athens, National Archaeological Museum.

S O U N I O N

USEFUL INFORMATION

Opening hours
Daily: 10.00 till sunset
Telephone: 0292 - 39 363

Part of the south colonnade of the temple of Poseidon. Despite the damage wrought by time and man, the monument preserves its vitality and splendour to a remarkable degree.

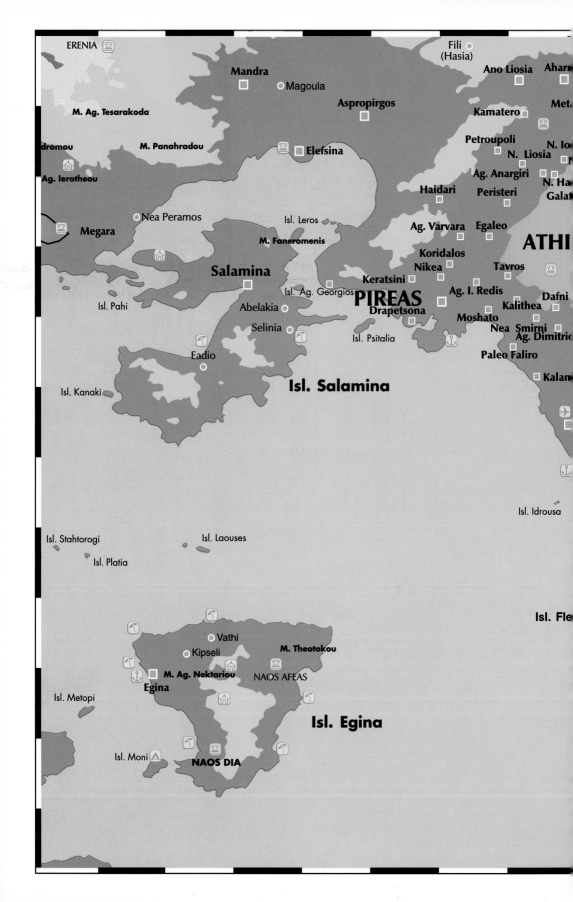

ERENIA

Mandra
Magoula
Aspropirgos

Fili
(Hasia)

Ano Liosia   Ahar
Met.
Kamatero
Petroupoli
N. Io
N. Liosia
Ag. Anargiri
N. Ha
Haidari   Peristeri   Galat

M. Ag. Tesarakoda

dromou   M. Panahradou   Elefsina
Ag. Ierotheou

Nea Peramos   Isl. Leros

Megara   M. Faneromenis

Salamina

Isl. Pahi   Isl. Ag. Georgios
Abelakia   PIREAS
Selinia   Drapetsona

Eadio

Isl. Kanaki   Isl. Salamina

Ag. Varvara   Egaleo   ATHI

Koridalos
Nikea   Tavros
Keratsini
Ag. I. Redis   Dafni
Kalithea
Moshato
Nea Smirni
Ag. Dimitri
Paleo Faliro
Kalan

Isl. Psitalia

Isl. Idrousa

Isl. Stahtorogi   Isl. Laouses
Isl. Platia

Isl. Fle

Vathi
Kipseli   M. Theotokou
M. Ag. Nektariou   NAOS AFEAS
Egina

Isl. Metopi   Isl. Egina

Isl. Moni   NAOS DIA

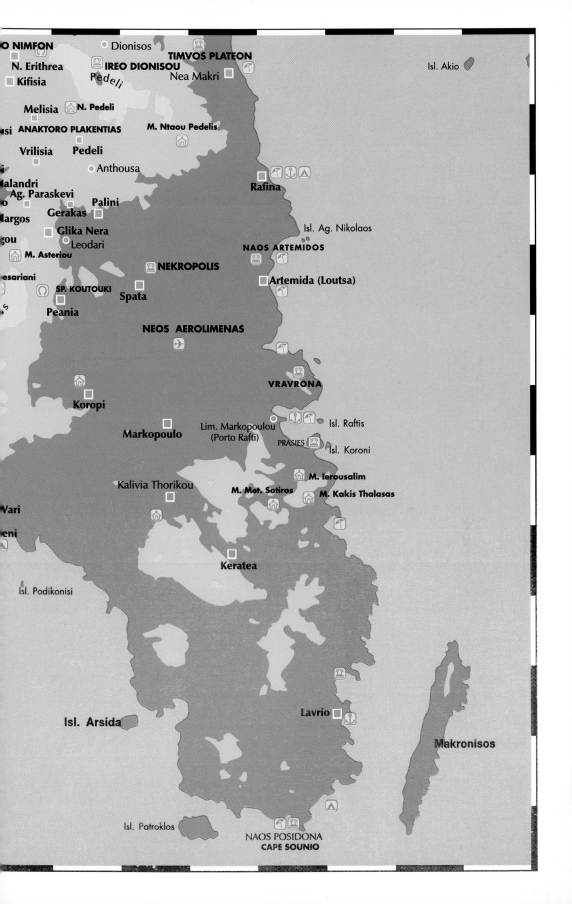

O NIMFON

Dionisos

N. Erithrea

TIMVOS PLATEON

IREO DIONISOU

Isl. Akio

Kifisia

Nea Makri

Pedeli

Melisia

N. Pedeli

ANAKTORO PLAKENTIAS

M. Ntaou Pedelis

Vrilisia

Pedeli

Anthousa

alandri

Ag. Paraskevi

Palini

Rafina

argos

Gerakas

Glika Nera

Isl. Ag. Nikolaos

ou

Leodari

NAOS ARTEMIDOS

M. Asteriou

NEKROPOLIS

Artemida (Loutsa)

esariani

SP. KOUTOUKI

Spata

Peania

NEOS AEROLIMENAS

VRAVRONA

Koropi

Lim. Markopoulou

Isl. Raftis

(Porto Rafti)

Markopoulo

PRASIES

Isl. Koroni

M. Ierousalim

Kalivia Thorikou

M. Met. Sotiros

M. Kakis Thalasas

Vari

eni

Keratea

Isl. Podikonisi

Isl. Arsida

Lavrio

Makronisos

Isl. Patroklos

NAOS POSIDONA

CAPE SOUNIO